MY

CONVERSATIONS

WITH

THE MISFITS

Litha M . Ndabula

Copyright © 2015 First Idea SA

ISBN: 978-1517316891

Published by First Idea®
© 2015 Litha M Ndabula
First Printing September 2015

To order additional copies of this resource visit www.firstideasa.com or email litha.ndabula@firstideasa.com

Printed in the Republic of South Africa
First Idea
Cape Town

CONTENTS

Preface   4

Prologue   7

Acknowledgements   8

CHAPTER 1   9

Brain and Mind Installation   9

Childhood —Peak of Our Creativity   17

Start Here – Lessons from my daughter   25

CHAPTER 2   30

TriuneBrainTheory   30

CHAPTER 3 - Poke the Box   38

Simon Brown – JustOneLap   38

Igor Marinkovic - Trading Wisdoms   86

Langa Mbulawa – Mbulawa & Sons   117

Lynette Barnes – Cape Honey Factory   132

CHAPTER 4 – The Juggernauts   153

Reuben Riffel – Reuben's Restaurants   153

Delane Zwane – Delacom Solutions   165

Greg Heasley – Naked Penguin Boy   193

Wongama Baleni – Department of Coffee   210

CHAPTER 5 – Here Be Dragons   237

Sizwe Nzima – Iyeza Express _   237

Lufefe Nomjana – Espinaca Innovations   271

CHAPTER 6 – There Were Lessons   301

PREFACE

Most of my working life has been nothing, but being obedient to the course set before me. Most of my days carried on going from one task to the next without bothering much to take time to look outside my daily routine. My tertiary days were nothing different to what most people get to experience, study, party, girls, etc. It was in the early summer of 2005, before doing my third year where for the first time I questioned the reason behind my waking up, catching a taxi to attend lectures. I was well aware that I needed a certificate to fit into society, as we now know it. The rude awakening was not about the certificate. I had asked myself that I would get the certificate after 3 years and then what would happen? In other words, I carried on attending lectures to attain a certificate, but that was not enough reason for me to get up every morning. At that point, against my parent's wishes, I reached a decision that I would start working fulltime in the same field I wanted to qualify in and continue to work study fulltime. This way, I would have to pay my own rent, buy own food, essentially being responsible for myself. Today, it is clear to me this was the start of my journey. Fear of me failing had gone from 1 to 9 on a scale of 0 to 10. I graduated a year later an average student in class. When I started writing this book, I was working for a state owned company where I dealt with a number of landowners. About a year I ago, I started showing interest in all the landowners I came across. Some of them were well off; others just managed to get by. Curiosity got the best of me and decided it would not hurt much to find out what they did for a living or how they got to their career of choice. What lay before me was an interesting revelation. These were individuals that had studied law and now run 2 to 5 commercial farms. They were engineers that left the engineering field to start up large international companies in other fields. I came across high school dropouts that became property developers in charge of some of the biggest developments in the country. Engineers had become fulltime stock market traders with no background in economics. These people were ahead of the average person and it pricked my curiosity. The questions grew within me, what, how, why?

Here were the individuals who have managed to do what most people and I have failed to do and that is using education as a tool to "**think & apply**." I soon learnt that they were waking up every morning to do something they loved; they were following their passion something most people struggle to find. In the current day as we know it, working is not about passion, but the need to earn a salary. It has become more about the need to fit into society, which is the one thing that is instilled in us for most of our childhood. We are told to go to school, get a degree, get a good job and get a career. Something that has worked well for a number of people some 50years ago, but does this really serves the majority of the population.

PROLOGUE

"Here's to the crazy ones. The misfits. The rebels. The troublemakers. The round pegs in the square holes. The ones who see things differently. They're not fond of rules. And they have no respect for the status quo. You can quote them, disagree with them, glorify or vilify them. About the only thing you can't do is ignore them. Because they change things. They push the human race forward. And while some may see them as the crazy ones, we see genius. Because the people who are crazy enough to think they can change the world, are the ones who do." – APPLE INC.

ACKNOWLEDGEMENTS

Great many thanks to those who have contributed in the writing of this book. A sincere word of gratitude goes to the entrepreneurs who gave up 60 minutes of their day to help share their experiences, weaknesses and strengths. They had no financial gain during and after the interviews, they have contributed out wanting to help others. Not to put any specific entrepreneur on a pedestal, but I would like to thank Langa Mbulawa, Delane Zwane, Simon Brown and Igor Marinkovic. These were the very first interviews that I did, had it not been for them I would have given up when the going got tough. The interviews have been kept in their original form and eight were conducted live. I would like to thank my wife, Tumi who read the first couple of interviews, my daughter Lwandle who was 5 years old at the time for reminding me how to think like a child.Finally, I would like to thank the following friends who gave guidance and suggested some potential candidates:

Tandikhaya Kubalo

Chris Epnaar

Martin Daniels

Luyanda Singenile

Makabongwe Mfengu

Antonio Coerecuis

Xola Vonya

CHAPTER ONE

Everyone is a genius. But if you judge a fish by its
ability to climb a tree, it will live its whole life
believing that it is stupid – Albert Einstein

Brain and Mind Installation

The start of a weekend was always something to look
forward to, staying at home with the family and
going for long drives on Saturdays that is when I was
lucky enough to have some spare change. This
feeling of excitement and freedom was always short
lived by the rush of anxiety attacks I would suffer
every Sunday evening. I could compare it to waking
up the day after Christmas and still think that there is
a slight chance that there will more be presents
under the Christmas tree. These painful episodes
were mostly caused by nothing other than the
thought of going back to work, by work I mean a
job; the one you dread to go to every morning. The
thought of sitting in that cubicle the whole day and
being micromanaged killed me with dread. I have
always known that I could do more and just how
much more, remained to be seen in the very bleak
future. The thought of leaving my full time job, take
time out before working again crossed my mind a
number of times. Sharing the thoughts with others

was probably the worst thing I ever did, I do not look down on those that shared advice with me. About 95% of the people who did had red lights going off as soon as I mentioned the idea and they could have easily ignited fear in me. For honesty's sake, some of them did ignite fear and I had to learn and find ways of overcoming that fear. I for one, have always been a dreamer and I have mostly chased those dreams. I looked around the office at people who had been doing the same job as me for the past 30 years; all of them were nowhere near to living the life I dreamt. I do not think I would forgive myself if I ever walked down that path. I had to uninstall everything I was taught as far as risk was concerned, forgetting about pulling out a spreadsheet that would make the power grid flick trying to see if I could afford my monthly expenses. I had to uninstall the fear that had been installed over the years in various ways.

The best way to understand this is to look at the brain as a computer and the mind as the software that gets installed. With most computers, the user gets the choice on what programs they would like to install for the computer to meet their needs. From time to time, they also get to choose what they no longer find useful and at times delete some programs. So is the human brain, what gets installed when we are young, is mostly enforced on us, and our abilities go as far as the programs installed. We are born with our brain already in our heads and since we have already survived 9 months in the womb knowing when to turn and stretch on our own, it is safe to say that we are born with the mind installed already; however limited. It is also safe to say that to a certain extent we are born with our own way of thinking. We come into the world knowing how to think be it crying when we want food or striving to crawl towards a toy that is on the floor, because we want it. Parents will know that kids will sometimes abuse this by crying for just about anything they want; this is creativity at best, innovation – using what you have to ascertain the desired outcome. No one teaches a child how to crawl, pick up a spoon and at times, we help the kids in some other way like supporting them with pillows to get them to learn how to sit early. We do not do this because we were brilliant enough to come up with the idea, it was taught to us somewhere back in the past. We are never instructed that one day we will have kids, this is how we should help them sit up, but we were able to retrieve this from deep within our central processing part of the brain. Put a toy in front of a child that is learning to crawl and watch how they will slowly try to slide towards that toy. The main reason is that they want; they have the sense to get what they want. In fact, any kid chases what they want until it hurts them, only then do they look elsewhere.

Unfortunately, by the time we are 3 years we lose our ability to think for ourselves. This is done through an enforced system of punishment and reward by our parents, guardians or even teachers. They are not aware of this; it is the way they have been raised by those before them. An example of how this works on the punishment side is that a child tries to cross the road without permission and the parent slaps the child on the wrist; they are trying to teach the child a lesson. This lesson stays with the child for the greater part of their life in the form of what I call a temporal paralysis. Millions of people around the globe live their lives without ever recovering from this state of paralysis and those who do soon climb to greater heights. Think of the last time you wanted to do something that made you happy and you stopped because you suddenly thought of the "suffering" this *might* cause. I have highlighted *might* because this is exactly how we look at each situation, and we have a bias in most. In the animal environment, a threat quickly passes and they move on, however with us humans we are more likely to spend most our lives in constant stressful situations that may never arrive. We start to imagine or experience stress just by imagining a stressful situation. Spanking a two-year-old child for crossing a road could make sense to some kids, but probably will not to most kids. We all know it is much safer to help them cross the road than to spank them. Take for an example of a kid that touches a hot stove, they will never do it again intentionally because they completely understand what dangers are associated with that. Again, this is a lesson they learn on their own; this is the punishment side.

On the reward side, I recall how my siblings and I would sit on the floor in a circle during meal times. We would go get our food from the kitchen and regroup in the form of a circle. It would be like a small eating tournament as everyone rushed to finish eating first regardless if you liked what was on that dish or not. The reason why we did this was that we knew the first person to finish would get an appraisal from the guardian in the form of applause and at times, they would get some candy. It is human nature to feel the need to compete, to be better and to stand out. This punishment and reward does have its minimal positive results, but at its best, it slowly erases our own way of thinking. We all know that when we cross the road, we observe our surroundings before doing so and not because we are reminded of the little spanking that we got when we were young; but because we want to be safe.

Let me delve more on some of my personal experience on the punishment side.

In my early schooling days, the teachers would make us line up outside the classroom and would give us a certain song to sing. The main purpose of this was to choose the "right" people for the choir. Now one of the much older women would walk slowly in front of us carefully listening to our voices. If she found that your voice was not good enough, she would immediately shout at you telling you that you are the main reason the choir sounded so bad. There were times comments like that would be followed by a smack on the face. You would be told to go back to the classroom, you cannot sing. Now we could argue that my voice was bad or not, but such actions would result in a child not wanting to ever sing even in the shower for that matter. You see, all I ever wanted to do was to be part of a choir and would listen to the Drakensburg Boys with my dad on some Friday evenings and imagine myself being part of a mass choir. Later while in high school I finally had the courage to try to join the choir once more, to my surprise, the teacher did not even want to listen to my voice. To my surprise, I was elected as a choir leader. My duties involved making sure everyone was present, we had all the notes. I thoroughly enjoyed it. The last night I sang in that choir I remember so vividly, it sounded all so romantic. The embarrassment I suffered as a kid caused me not to think about doing something I wanted, it acted as a barrier for the greater part of my school life. I certainly do not blame the teacher, if anything I blamed the process in which we were being taught, the current way of educating and dealing with kids. There was one way of dealing with this dilemma I faced, simply uninstall the corrupted software in my brain and give being part of a choir yet another attempt.

While doing Grade 9, we went on a tour to the then city of Port Elizabeth. Part of the school tour would be to go to the University of Port Elizabeth where would undergo some psychometric valuation. The main purpose for this was to help us choose the right career path. I still recall the school's headmaster informing us how most people choose the wrong career path and later ended up unhappy with the path they had chosen. To me this made a lot of sense, I think any Grade 9 learner would have jumped at the chance; I saw this as an opportunity of a lifetime. Before the visit to the university, I was crazy about Business Economic and Accounting as school subjects and I did quite well in them. A part of me believed at the time that I would pursue a career in the line of economics. The valuation took two days; we had follow up sessions with the psychologists where they would share the results. I can recall how the good lady described me as someone who liked to do filing and kept tidy. She then told me I should pursue a career in law and she did this from reading what I wrote; somewhere in there, I mentioned that I liked keeping records of my belongings. I discussed with her how I liked accounting and business economics as studies. She told me that I could study something in that line, but I would later suffer in my studies as a result. When I went back to school after that with thoughts of becoming a lawyer and make no doubt about it I did not even challenge the new revelation in my life. It rolled out over the preceding weeks in a number of ways and the most obvious one was that I lost interest in accounting and business economics, to this date I have no clue what I gained interest in. I dropped the two subjects in high school because of this new information, but still had no idea what I wanted to study. Some 16years later, I still have not figured out what the psychologist came up with, but it would happen that 10 years later I stumbled across the stock market. I came across some of the most beautiful acronyms I ever heard of in any career and they were things like EV/EBITDA, WACC, PEG, CAPEX, just to name a few. I immediately fell in love with it all and started educating myself. I read books, attended seminars, could with reasonable degree compile a spreadsheet and focus stock prices. With time, I realized that to some extent I managed to gain back my love for economics and accounting, but also realized that once again I managed to uninstall what had been installed in the past. The problem is that it took me about 8 years to do the uninstalling when I tried to get in the choir, it took me 10years to uninstall what I was told by the psychologist; we may not always have that time to pursue what we want.

What I will focus on the most in the upcoming pages is a way I believe we can all combat this and fight for what be we believe we can achieve.

CHILDHOOD – THE PEAK OF OUR CREATIVITY

From a very young age, we are groomed to achieve something in life and in some of these cases, this is desirable to the guardian. Where I grew up what I would hear the most is what a parent wanted their child to be when they grow up. I remember one instance where the mother forced the child to go to a medical school and the result was that the child spent six good years of his life failing miserably; eventually they excluded him from the university. The years following that the child, now a young man went on to study electrical engineering and today runs his own company. The question to ask around here was this in the very least evident when the child was growing up? Bill Gates, the founder of Microsoft was also one of the people forced by his parents to study law, although at the age of 12, he was already showing a lot of enthusiasm in technology. One of the attributing factors to this was off course that these careers were the most respectable career paths in the past. There was a time in my primary school days where almost everyone in the class wanted to be a doctor and to this very day, I do not know of any of my former classmates that are doctors. We all wanted this because at the time we saw doctors as the most successful people although we could not even stand the sight of blood. Are doctors the most successful people, probably not, but we were fixated on the idea. Most of what we believe to be true is not necessarily true. Over the years, we have gone from a species that questioned a number of things ranging from our existence to how we breathe, to accepting what we perceive to be a norm. We have gone from a species of discovering gravity, designing ways to transport humans in the air to being just passengers. Today we board airplanes to get to our next destination without as much as thinking how the first airplane came about. Something had to happen for this change to take place and a lot of it goes to what Ken Robinson calls Changing the Education Paradigms. We are slowly educating people out of creativity and robbing them out of their ability to think. The current way in which we are educating people, was designed for the industrial age when mines, railways and buildings went up as fast as smartphones pop up these days. We educate kids to conform; we groom them so that they are accepted by society, as we know it. We take these kids and put them in rows as they would sit products in the factory, we give them batch numbers and if they are defective at the end of this process, we send them back to start all over. We ring bells to tell them when they can rest and for how long, we put them through the grinding mill in the classroom without first understanding their needs. Then there are those whom we label as ADHD or some dyslexic when they cannot comply with the norm, yet study shows that people who are dyslexic are likely to do much better later in life than those who are not. Below is a list of dollar millionaires who suffered from dyslexia

1.	Henry Ford Companies	Ford	Motor
2.	Ingvar Kamprad	IKEA	
3.	Rirchard C Strauss Developer	Real	Estate
4.	Charles Schwab	Charles Schwab	
5.	Richard Branson	Virgin	
6.	William Hewlett	HP	
7.	Steve Jobs	Apple	
8.	Steven Spielberg	Dream Works	
9.	Tommy Hilfiger	Hilfiger Clothing	

10. Walt Disney   Walt   Disney
Company

When we find kids suffering from this we continue to find ways to change them, feed them medication and we claim that they cannot put things in order and I guess the question here is whose order? I am not denying the fact that they struggle to read and need aiding. Many of us are only able to write all 26 alphabets, in one order and in truth, some would not have known that the exact number of alphabets is 26 in total until they read this. We were all taught to write them in one order A – Z and we were all taught to write 1 -10. The later makes sense 10 is bigger than 1, but how about Z, is it bigger than A? I have spent time trying to find why alphabets are listed the way they are and the only close answer was that it was easy to memorize. I recently went to a parent's meeting at my daughter's school and discovered that the first alphabet they teach kids is the letter V, only because it is easy to write. When I went to school corporal punishment was still very much in use and asking this question then would have somehow earned me a good hiding. If you think my theory might not necessarily hold I challenge you to put this book down, grab a piece of paper and a pen and write all the alphabets in no alphabetical order; do not try to recall them in their alphabetical order as you write them. Most teachers will impart this knowledge to the kids, without knowing what they are doing, without having the answers to these questions.

I grew up in South Africa, small town with no traffic lights, no cinemas. Why even mention cinemas, there was no electricity, most TV sets were run off from car batteries. I recall in the evenings how we would sit around a lantern light and make shadow puppets on the wall, how we would use steel wire to build cars we would drive around the dusty streets. Pals of mine that were really good at it would design shapes which had resemblance to the Mercedes Benz the rich folks had at the time. We made soccer balls using old sack bags that were used for packaging onions and oranges. After watching the then famous series MacGyver, we would gather as boys and grab small wooden sticks we used as guns and we would act out scenes from the series. I can never forget my favorite one, which is how I learnt to play pool table. My parents were very strict and I was not allowed to be within a couple of yards of the Pub doors. Therefore, friends of mine started digging six holes into the ground about 50cm in length, using off cuts from a local timber place and would nail the wood in the ground; these were to become the sides of our "pool table". We went around town picking old Coca-Cola bottle caps, red and white, and these would become the pool balls. The thought of how I learnt to play pool always floods my mind every time I play on a real pool table. In a nutshell, my childhood was filled with artists that could do animation, draw comic books, design and build cars, puppeteers, etc. Our imagination ran wild. All of a sudden, shadows became just shadows, clay became just dirt, and steel-wire….what was that again? When I grew up, Legos were used to build anything your mind could imagine. Today we buy Legos for our kids and on the outside of the box there is a picture specific to only what can be built with the pieces. A number of factors that caused us to be ignorant; but at the top of the list is the way we are currently educated from home, society and school. We learn how to memorize, to keep our school uniform clean and no more playing with clay. I remember a close friend in Grade 5 received corporal punishment because at the back of his history book he drew pictures. Why not let kids learn what they really show interest in, why do we continue to kill creativity?

3 years ago, I was raising a Labrador puppy and I have raised dogs before with the help of my dad, this was the first one I would raise all by myself. I had to get some info on how I would go about this and what was the best way of dealing with this than consulting the internet. One of the few things I

learnt is that they like to play and biting things and the fact that they can be very messy. One important thing I learnt was with their biting and that I should be careful not to hit him when he grabs on things because he will start to think that it is wrong. The result of this is that the dog would think that biting is wrong and therefore never bite again. It is interesting that there was so much information on the internet about guiding a dog the right direction and yet little about kids. In retrospect, I do not recall searching the internet for information when my child was born, when she started walking or when she went to school. Those are the things I immediately think I could easily handle because I have seen kids being raised up in the past.

A practical approach on how this approach could affect a child

I am resting on the couch one Saturday afternoon after a tough day doing some garden work and my daughter shouts from the room asking what numbers make up the number 10. I yelled back at her that it is "1" and "0". She came rushing in the lounge with a piece of paper wanting to know if she got it right and she held the paper in front of her and all I could see is what is shown on the image.

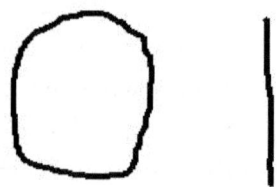

There are two possible answers to this and the most obvious answer would have been to tell her that she is wrong and that 1 should come before the 0. The second answer I would be required to do a bit more thinking from my side; what are the chances that she wrote it correctly, but rotated the paper when she came to show me. What would be the long-term implication of me telling her she is wrong instead of putting a bit more effort on my side to see this from all sides? This kind of quick thinking or response goes as far as the companies we get employed by. I recall a particular instance at a company I worked for where there was a complaint from a client on project I worked on. I was in charge of the groundwork while the decisions came from high above and on this particular project, someone gave the go ahead without consulting me if the paperwork was all in order. The manager came storming in the office not to find out what had happened, but to give me a serious lecture, there could have been two solutions to this. The long-term repercussions of the way this was handled could result in a number of things from being disgruntled, a go slow to even a negative attitude about the work in general.

START HERE"- LESSONS FROM MY 5 YEAR OLD DAUGHTER

Firstly, I must say working on First Idea from when it was just a thought to launching it has had a number of valuable lessons in my life. To name but a few I can start by the planning stages, what I wanted at first, how that evolved, the people I have met and have given me time in their lives to interview them. There were some challenges after the first four interviews and I was highly motivated by them to overcome. At some point, I started questioning a number of things and as crazy as it may sound, I started questioning what is actually real and what is not. Most of what we believe to be real is not necessarily always the case no matter how we try to force our minds to believing it is.

One example of this is fear, what do we fear the most, failure, fear of the unknown, fear of rejection. Unfortunately, for us as humans the thought of an event occurring is good enough to ignite fear, even if the event is in the future. Therefore, is it real or is it something that our minds become accustomed to over time. I wake up every morning and stress about future events like business not being good enough, fear of not succeeding, fear of financial security and at times even death itself. Sure thing, death is real, but do I really need to fear it because I could collapse while writing this; I hope that is not the case, but we fear over things we absolutely have no control over and it does ruin the moment for most of us. On the other hand, I watch my 5 year old daughter getting up in the morning and excited about her birthday, which is in 4 months' time, and every day she speaks with the same level of enthusiasm about her upcoming birthday. I know at times she dreads to wake up in the morning and go to school, but I have never heard her moaning about the getting up the night before. On the other hand, I stress about not being able to afford her birthday present in 4 months' time. Is this real, or is it all a choice?

Time for me get to the main point, which is how much of what we are taught at home or school is actually true when it comes to decision making. How much of it do we believe and see the relevance of in our everyday thinking. Most of us did a bit of mathematics in school (I would like to believe) and know that 1+1= 2. Mathematics is about solving problems, train the brain to think and work at problems. I have moaned about why was I taught y = mx +c as I have never used this in my working life and the answer is simple, what I believed or thought to be true was actually not the case. I do not recall being told why I needed to study mathematics, except that it is a required subject to be able to do an engineering course at a tertiary level. The important lesson left out here was how it was supposed to train my brain to solve problems. At this very stage, what we are hearing from successful entrepreneurs is to come up with business ideas that solve the problems of the community, and then the money will follow. We have all the skill sets required for this and we have been acquiring them for years.

The heading is **"Start Here - Lessons from my 5year old daughter"** and a couple of months ago she asked me to help her solve the maze puzzle below as I was about to take my midday nap. She held the crayon at the center of the page and first thing that came to mind when I saw the puzzle was the writing "Start Here" on the left side of the paper. I indicated to her that she should not start from the center and the second time I was getting slightly agitated; she insisted on starting from the center. Now having worked on this book already by then, I quickly said hang on, what am I doing here. She wanted to do it differently and to me it was her own unique way; needless to say that she solved the puzzle in less than 20 seconds, doing so in her own way. That is what successful entrepreneurs do, they do things in their own unique way, and they do not follow the status quo. The educated me on the other hand, was trying to make her follow the norm, what is expected of her. To a certain degree I was convinced on what was not real "Start here" and ignoring the fact that there were two solutions to the problem at hand. One might argue that she will never know where to start, but I think the whole point of the maze is to connect the two points. The "Start Here" mentality plays a crucial role as the rest of our lives pan by, especially when we choose our careers. One studies Information Technology and thinks that the only right thing to do is to start an IT company. Jack Ma was a teacher before he founded Alibaba, Bill Gates went to varsity to study law, Giorgio Armani was in a medical school before he dropped out, Kerryne Krause-Neufeldt began a career with honors in Communication before branching into technology-based cosmetic products.

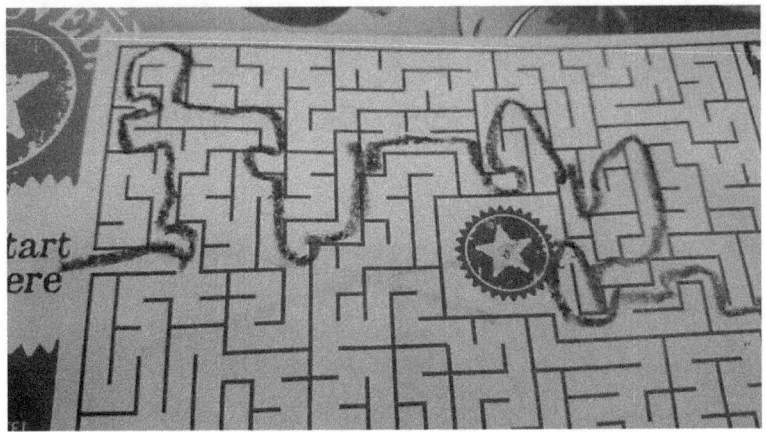

CHAPTER TWO

Triune Brain Theory – Dr. Paul Mclean

Dr. Paul Maclean was a neuroscientist and psychiatrist and became known for amongst other things the Triune Brain Theory in the 1950s. He spent time studying the brain's control over emotions and behavior. He began his experiment with animals, would study the animal's reactions to certain stimulus, which included sexual arousal and aggression.

After conducting the first two interviews, I started looking for key similarities between the two interviewees; I wanted to find that one thing they had in common. What I found was that both individuals had to make an important decision at some point in their lives; this was about stepping out of their comfort zone. Dr. Maclean called the center of the brain as the limbic brain and this was the part that reacted to emotions be it pleasurable or painful sensations. Later in the 1960s, he took this theory further to humans where he called the area that dealt with survival the R-complex (lizard brain), limbic brain dealt with the emotions and the neocortex dealt with reasoning and creativity.

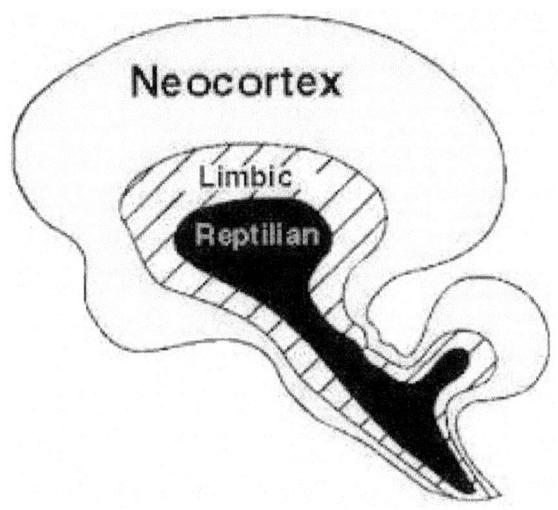

Reptilian/ Lizard Brain/ R-complex

This part of the brain has a number of names and I prefer using the lizard brain, it makes more sense and it is easy to remember. The lizard brain is the protective part of the brain that deals with survival. If you have ever come across a lizard, the first thing it normally does is to run away even though you mean it no harm. The same applies to a number of animals like birds or a rabbit; the first thing that comes to mind is survival, fight or flight. Animals are known to be equipped with only this part of the brain and for humans, this is one of three. For humans this part of the brain sits on top of the spinal cord and that is where the nerve senses come through to get to the brain. If you recall the last time you burnt your finger, how quick you were able to remove it, that was your lizard brain in charge. In the old days, a man would continue having babies until a male heir is born to take on the family name, the man might not be alive to see this happen, but they would believe in it nonetheless. If this did not happen, they would even go as far as marrying another woman to make sure a male heir was born; this applied more in the days where nations were under the rule of kings. This was the lizard brain in play fighting or survival. Over the years, this has evolved to control human behavior more and acts as a limiting factor, decisions have become based on the lizard brain now more than ever. The lizard brain has become the driving force behind our fears. One day you have a brilliant business idea you would like to try out and the lizard brain takes charge and cuts you down to your size. We cannot function until we are able to control this.

Limbic Brain

The limbic brain only exists in humans and is the part of the brain which is responsible for emotions, sensations, be it pleasurable or painful. A simple way to look at this is to think of the last time it was blazing hot and you had an ice cold Coca-Cola. The emotions that go with quenching that thirst engrave a feeling in our limbic brain that associates an ice cold Coca-Cola with hot temperatures. This goes as far as emotions attached to paydays at a place of employment, 13th cheque at the end of the year or even the bank balance. You have a unique business idea and you cannot start because your limbic brain controls your healthy bank balance or tells you to wait for the 13th cheque. What is even more lethal is the combination of the lizard and limbic brain working together. As humans, we make decisions based on the two and this does not always provide clear thinking. An example is someone who is in an abusive relationship; they will always want to leave, but the emotional attachment and fear of starting over causes them to stay anyway. The same applies to working conditions that are not conducive to one's future; we fear more of what may come than what is currently happening now. If you have ever chased a stray animal from your yard you will know that eventually it will show up again; the reason is that animals do not have a limbic brain. Whereas if you chase a human being away or cause any harm to them, they will remember it and most probably will hold it against you.

Neocortex

This is the outer part of the brain and is the thinking, intelligence, creative and reasoning part of the brain. Humans are the only mammals that are equipped with this and largely fail to use it. We think mostly using the first two parts and not the neorcotex. Creativity is most evident in our childhood days and slowly erodes, as we get older because we start to learn of things like risk and failure. Kids are hardly aware of failure and I remember my daughter would bring me a broken toy and she would ask me to fix it. The toy would be in an irreparable state, but she did not see it that way. People who have managed to achieve great success following their passion and tried new things have managed to do what most of us cannot do. They have managed to regain their way of thinking by blocking the lizard and limbic brain, only thinking with their neorcotex when planning. They do not let fear or emotions hinder their thought and decision making process. An ordinary average person will see failure as a sign to quit; while these few individuals see it as a lesson. When we fail, we only have a lesson to learn, we only fail when we do not learn a lesson. To get to think the way these people think, we have one and only one thing to do, that is to admit that we are crazy. We have to admit that we have completely lost our own way of thinking due to external influences primarily the learning process. In order to get this right, we would need to question our decision-making process constantly finding out if we are making them based on fear or emotions.

I have gone around the country interviewed 10 entrepreneurs whom I believe they have managed to unlock this. There were some entrepreneurs that were rejected by tertiary institutions, some found their passion after having worked in other career fields for years and others simply dropped out to pursue their passion. What is important to note is that this is not about how much they have or make, it is simply about their way of thinking. We cannot change who they are or how they do things; look for similarities rather than differences to your current struggle. I was more interested in their struggles, their triumphs and problem solving skills. While reading the interviews take moments to pause and see how you would have solved some of the problems they faced at some point in their lives.

The descriptions of the chapter titles:

POKE THE BOX

These individuals have managed to get a tertiary qualification or two, but found their passion in another field of work. They were not limited by what they studied and achieved great things in just being driven by their passion. They were not afraid to Poke the Box.

THE JUGGERNAUTS

These individuals did not hold a tertiary qualification and could have been rejected by the education standards. They did not let this to be a limiting factor in their chase for success and would let nothing stand in their way. A juggernaut, a force regarded mercilessly destructive and unstoppable.

HERE BE DRAGONS

Means unexplored territory, these were individuals who were not afraid to change things or wonder off unexplored lines. They could have been rejected by the current education system and managed to tap deep into their passion. As a result, they have managed to land a spot in Forbes 30 under 30 promising entrepreneurs in Africa.

As a point of interest, here is a list of rich people whom I believe have also unlocked the true potential of the neorcotex:

1. Oprah Winfrey – fired from her first television job as an anchor in Baltimore.

2. Steven Spielberg – he was rejected by a university multiple times.
3. Theodor Seuss – he was rejected by 27 different publishers.
4. Jack Ma – rejected by Harvard University 10 times.
5. Henry Ford – had a reputation for failed automobile businesses.
6. Sir James Dyson – went through 5126 failed prototypes when he was inventing a vacuum.
7. Colonel Sanders – the founder of KFC was fired from a number of jobs before he started the company.

CHAPTER THREE

Poke The Box

Your art is what you do when no one can tell you
exactly how to do it. Your art is the act of taking
personal responsibility, challenging the status quo, and
changing people.— Seth Godin

SIMON BROWN   OF **JUSTONELAP**

INTRODUCTION: I first came across Simon at an
investing seminar in Cape Town and he was presenting
there. Something kept on drawing me to his
presentations, which would take place about three
times each quarter. Simon had the ability to get the
message heard and when I left his presentations, I
could definitely remember most of the things he said.
Simon appeared to be a relaxed individual and I would
sometimes throw in some questions at him over a glass
of wine. At the time, I had just entered the world of
stock trading and I felt like some help could come from
this gent. I soon noticed his face was on quite a number
of places like SA Warrants, Business Day TV, CNCBC
Africa, Maude Street. I started to hear his voice on
radio and that is when I realized he was quite a busy
man, he appeared calm, but very busy. What stood out
the most for me during the seminars was the concept
of "lazy working."

===*Simon can you share a bit of background about yourself*===

I am from KZN. I lived all over the place; I think we moved twenty times before I was 10years old. I was born in Bulwer; I lived in Hluhlulwe, Mhlanga, south coast, inland and all over the place. By the age of 10, my parents were divorced and moved to Pinetown. I finished my schooling in Pinetown, including my junior school. I went to Pinetown Boystown Boys High and matriculated in 1987. I then went to Natal Technikon to do film and video production; I studied film and video for 3years. I went to Cape Town in 1990 because I needed to do practical work in film & video to complete the diploma. I lived there for about 3–4years; I was supposed to start a job in London, but had a very bad motorbike accident ten days before that; London was out and I ended back in Durban where I met my current wife. She was moving to Maritzburg, so I went there. I moved to Jo'burg in 2007 to start working at Standard Online Share Trading and left that end of 2010 to start JustOneLap

If I go back to what I was doing in that time; so in Cape Town I was doing film & video for a bit, then we launched an extreme sport magazine. These days the idea of mountain biking, paragliding, bungee jumping and other stuff is probably a lot more out there, but back then around 1991 it was not so popular. There was no internet in those days; I mean there was CompuServe but no internet. Launched that, but it did not work. I had a little publishing company that kind of muddled along and paid the bills. I went to Maritzburg and then to Durban. There was no job in Durban; well I managed some restaurants and stuff. I have always gone back to restaurants for me it was an easy way to make money either as a waiter, manager, chef or something like that. I have always found that as my out, when I needed a job desperately, I would go and find a restaurant to work at. In Maritzburg, odd enough I worked for Ster-Kinekor for a year as a regional manager for the internal cinemas, which sounded fancy, but there were only two and both were in Pietermaritzburg. I left that, got involved in publishing but this time differently. Not publishing, rather importing, getting the rights to international lists, bringing them into South Africa and then distributing them to bookshops locally. That also included other companies that had rights to South Africa I would then manage the Kwazulu-Natal aspects. So I was basically going to bookshops, selling those books and the like. That's because I love books, I have got a library in the room next door with 5000 books. Then I started getting involved in the stock market at that point. I had been in the market for a long time and we can delve into that in more detail, but I started trading in the mid-90s losing money spectacularly. I started trading geared products, warrants in '97 and just lost money faster. Because I was trading warrants and I was one of the few people who actually understood them and had spent time learning about them; I was on the internet. I was early to the internet, chat forums and that sort of stuff. So I launched two websites, one was SA Review which did not work. The idea behind that were book reviews, movie reviews and restaurant reviews. Perhaps if I had put more time to it, it is still a concept and we see it out there, it is everywhere. The other one was SA Warrants, because I had become sort of the retail expect in the warrants space. This was obviously Dot-com boom, warrants offered gearing. Didata share price goes from R7 to R70, add gearing to that, you make or lose a fortune. And then I launched a website 20th March 2000, I remember that because the 21st of March is a public holiday off course these days. I launched it in March the 20th and it just exploded. It just took off and was hugely popular. Literally, within a week, I had 4-5 offers on the table and I did not really want to sell it because my revenue was still coming from publishing. This was just a hobby on the side. So I didn't really want to sell it and I got approached by two guys that were running a website called Money Tech. They did not want to buy the website; they said they would give me R3000 a month and in 2000 that bought a lot of wine. They did not want to own the website; all I had to do was to associate with them, be on their chat forum. They would have a subscription service and I would have to issue a buy and sell recommendation on the subscription service. I am like this is free money so off course I agree and at about the same time I ended up on the front page of the Business Times with a screaming headline "HOW TO TRIPLE YOUR MONEY IN 3 MONTHS" or something like that. Which was hindsight, I had not done it and I had not claimed to have done it I just showed an example of how to use a call and put warrant; what you could have done in Didata and how you could have with perfect timing tripled your money. My website exploded, I forget the exact numbers, but I did more traffic on one Sunday than I had done in the entire preceding month type of scenario. I had people phoning; a woman from Newcastle phoned me asking what's your bank account I want to send money and I am like who are you?? So then I started doing this more seriously and I started doing a lot more teaching. I have always enjoyed public speaking; as a kid I had bad speech impediments I could not say my "M and S" and stuff. So my mother had sent me to speech and drama sessions. Then I started with SA Warrants not doing very well, we tied up with Money Max, which ultimately became Fin24.com owned by Mweb, ultimately owned by Naspers. We hooked up with them and that gave us a nice market; we started doing courses and the like. I had a partner; I was still based in Botha's Hill running SA Warrants and doing well. We did courses, subscription services; we had adverts and doing very,

very well. The problem is that we were a giant fish in a tiny pond. We dominated our niche, but it was a tiny, tiny niche and I had gotten into a bit of a rapt in day trading, it had worked and stuff. I had been doing some work for Standard Online Share Trading, the chap who ran it at the time called Richard Seddon doing some training for them and the like. In truth, I kept on trying to sell them advertising and they never bought the advertising; but kept on offering me more training work. I was happy to do it; I was flying around the country doing presentations around investing, trading and managing your money etcetera, to their client base. In 2006, he phoned me a couple of times to offer me a job in Johannesburg and the idea of Joburg did not appeal to me. I lived on 10000square meters of land on top of the hill at Botha's Hill and my closest neighbour was on the other side of the hill; I had eagles in the valley and owls in the trees. Then something happened he phoned later in that year and I thought, let us go to Joburg. I checked with my wife and she was having a tough time at her job, she was the Head of Department Sociology in Pietermaritzburg. So we came to Joburg, moved here 1st Feb 2007. I worked for Online Share Trading for 4years running their training education internal and external. By then I had a reputation for someone who knew what he was doing, also for someone who knew how to teach. At my core I am a teacher, nothing fancy, I am just a teacher. I then decided that I want to start JustOneLap and the premise behind JustOneLap is to teach people about money; everything from budgeting, to investing, to trading high risk derivative products. The key thing was it was rich. The problem with doing face to face courses is that you do not go to Polokwane very often and you go to Bizana even less frequently, KwaNdengezi you never get to. So it had to be online, the internet does two things, it removes time and geography in that I can log on and communicate with someone anywhere in the world, so geography is removed from the equation. In addition, at the same time, I can leave a message for them via email, via video and they come to it whenever they want. We now have PVR on our decoders and we understand the concept, but back in the day, this was radical. You know if we go back to early 2000 this was completely new. I play correspondence chess online; I used to do it with postcards, now I play up to 150 games at a time with people all over the world. That is what JustOneLap was going to do, to take quality information, disseminate globally although South Africa primarily and Africa as an interest, but South Africa as my focus. Make it quality, make it available to anyone with internet access and most importantly, make it free. A lot of folks say if it is free, it's no good and I hear what they are saying. The truth of the matter is that if I put a price, I put a barrier no matter what that price is; whether the price is R10, R1000 or R10000, if I put a price, I immediately put a barrier and that will stop a significant number of people from coming through. Firstly, because people might not have R10; secondly they might not have a way to pay you R10; thirdly because we all know it, we are on the net we are having a great time and suddenly we get to a pay wall and then we stop. 99 times out of a hundred we reverse, we hit that pay wall and we say we will find it somewhere else. So it had to be free and the model is then Third Parties sponsor the website the likes of the JSE, IG Markets, Standard Bank, etcetera and that is where the revenue comes. So that is what I had been doing since January 2011 having left Standard Bank. I am still based in Johannesburg although still travelling. I do JustOneLap, work for Standard Online Share Trading still. I work for the JSE with their Powerhours, I do columns for Finweek, and I do TV shows on Business Day TV. I run Maude Street, which is currently on the shelf taking a holiday it will be back in January, which is a weekly podcast. I think that is all I do.

===*Simon, going back to when you chose Film & Video, was that something that you were crazy about*===

I am going to be honest and say no, there is a story behind it. I finished school in 1987, as a white male I had to go do 2years of national service. There was no way on earth I was going to go and do 2years of national service; it was just not going to happen and I did not support it. There were limited options to me, I could live the country, but at that point, we thought I could never return. I could hide or I could stay in varsity and you just had to study. I actually applied to do journalism and I wanted to do journalism within the financial space. There was at that point in the Mail & Gurdian (although back then it was still called the Weekly Mail) a chap called Thomas Equinus who wrote a horse racing column. I do not give a hoot about horseracing, but it was the first thing I read every week because it was brilliant writing. I thought I want to do brilliant, insightful person on the street writing, but I want to do it in the finance space. So I went to tech and applied. I also applied at Rhodes, but I failed matric and could not get into university. When I went to Tech, you are sitting there in the interview process; they said to me what sort of journalist do you want to be? I said to them I want to be the best financial journalist there is and I could just see them. Their eyes glazed up, so they rejected me. I discovered there was a new course Film & Video. I am interested in photography; it is not a passion of mine. I had not been making movies, it is not a passion of mine, and I like watching movies. I mean who does not I am a teenager. On an off chance, I applied partly because I desperately needed to. This is like October '87 if I was not accepted into something very soon; I would have had to leave the country. So I applied for Film & Video and they accepted me. I am gob smacked, but hey what the hell. So off I went and spent 3 years doing it and I loved it. I had learnt a huge amount particularly from the practical side on how to edit, how to build suspense without special effects and just good old-fashioned video making; I loved it, I thoroughly enjoyed it. I worked in it a couple of years in Cape Town and I think my next career if anything, I always say when I grow up I want to be a photographer. That is probably what I want to do next. I mean I learnt stuff that I use now, I am making videos now and I am doing audio work; they are going online although they are not movies, they are educational videos. There are things I learnt there, but it was not my passion.

===*Simon, you do a lot of public speaking these days. You mentioned earlier that you had to attend special speech classes, has this benefitted you when you look back*===

They certainly did. I am cognitively dyslexic and I could not read when I was 7years old. I remember that because I was at a school in Warmer Beach, which is south of Durban, south of Toti. I could not read and none of my teachers realised how bad it was because I kept on moving. Every 3 – 4 months my father would get a new job and I would have to go to a new school. So none of the teachers fully comprehended how bad it was. In truth if someone had not picked it up, I would have been in deep, deep trouble. I then moved to a school I think it was Waterfall in KZN just outside Hillcrest. I came across a brilliant teacher who immediately knew what my problem was. She immediately knew what to do to help with dyslexia and the like. So she very quickly got me through to a point where I read a hundred books a year and in truth I scheme read some of them. A hundred books a year that is not fast enough, books are coming at me faster than I can read them. What that did is it put me in front of people and make no mistake when I did my first presentation via SA Warrants in 2003 was probably the scariest thing of my life, but I knew that I had the background to it and that I could do it. I am still cognitively dyslexic and I still struggle to read. I have thought myself a cheat where I look at the shape of the word rather than the letters and it typically works, but it has some faults sometimes.

===you have also mentioned something about a magazine that you started. That is quite different from what you studied, can you share the thinking behind such a move===

At the end I am a serial entrepreneur, I started my first business when I was 5 years old and I sold it to my sister when I was 6years. I start businesses. The reason it was a magazine, I will be perfectly honest, I am in Cape Town, the company I am working for doing video editing closes down or they closed their Cape Town offices and offered me a job in Joburg. I declined; I mean I am in Cape Town, why come live in Joburg. I am living in a house with a bunch of other folks who are designing menus, flyers and stuff like that. We had a brainstorming session one night and the one guy was doing parachuting and we say hey, there might something here. So we do not do any marketing, we just sort of go barreling in and kind of start this process. We were completely ignorant of it, but the idea of extreme sport was obviously fun and exciting. We could see the growth projection happening. I had been working at a production company, we had done an advert for Hi-Tec shoes, and we had bought some kiwis out to do bungee jumping because the Kiwis were going around the country charging people to jump off bridges. It all just rather fitted and that is often how it is; you kind of fall into stuff. I mean with SA Warrants, I kind of fell into it. If I hadn't had that front page of Business Times, it would have been just a little hobby that went nowhere. I have no idea where I would be sitting today.

===*so you eventually left the Mother City to come to Joburg, has the decision paid off in terms of your career*==

Without a shadow of a doubt! I mean when I was sitting in Botha's Hill running SA Warrants and day trading having a very lazy, pleasant, enjoyable life, surfing a lot, walking dogs and drinking wine; I dominated a niche. I was struggling with how to leave that niche to find a new pond, a new place to go; you know you are a giant fish in a tiny pond. Standard Bank did a number of things, it brought me to Joburg, and it brought me right to the heart of the industry. It gave me a bit of legitimacy that I am now working for one of the biggest banks in the continent. Coincidently 5months after I joined Standard Bank, CNBC launches CNBC Africa so I start doing commentary there. They are putting me in front because of the classes I am doing with thousands of their clients every year. I did not say yes to the jobs because I had this all plotted out as it is often the case. You say yes, then you do something and there are a whole lot of implications that happen, that in this case were all positive. It leapfrogged me make no mistake about it, it absolutely leapfrogged me so that when I left Standard Bank 4years later I had a reputation and a name; so that if I phoned people, they knew who I was. I had proved to people that I could do what I said I could do etcetera. So it was hugely important.

===*the move to Standard Bank was quite a different one, did this have any special courses in terms of what you were going to do there or you just sort of tagged along with what was happening*===

Yes I did. It is one of the great things about working for a large corporate is that they will spend money on staff education and the like. I did a couple of courses around presenting techniques and sometimes you leave /have learnt anything. Sometimes a 5-minute session leapfrogs you forward type of scenario. It did a lot mostly around public speaking, presenting, TV technique, radio technique and hostile interviews. I went on their global course, which is a two-week long course that they offer for their staff. Then just a huge amount of trying to understand how people learn, from a teacher's perspective, how does the brain work. There is two parts to it and one is how do we spend our money. The secret to wealth is that there is no secret; we know how to get rich which is spend less than you earn, done, it is as simple as that. However, we don't and why don't we? So it's trying to understand how the brain is working in terms of the decisions and responses we make in terms of our life, which for me is focusing on money; obviously this is broader it's careers, relationships and everything else. It is also trying to understand how people learn so that when I am doing presentations and the like, I am getting stuff into their heads. A lot of what we think is how we learn is actually not the case, we think it is about repetition and it is not. We think it is about reading the same thing ten times and it is not. What it is actually doing is that the harder the experience, the more likely you are to learn. Quick tangent, the best way we learn is you make it hard. You read something that is difficult and then you come back to it about 6 months later with like a snap test or something like that. It is hard to retrieve it, but the fact is that you do retrieve and that act of retrieval actually entrenches the memory. Then again in

6 months or a year later, you use it again, but you are using it almost casually now. Now you are pulling up that memory up at will. As a quick analogy, your parent teaches you how to tie knots and it's difficult, but you learn how to tie knots. Then many years later you go camping and you actually need to tie some knots. You reach deep in your memory bank, you pull out that memory, you tie those knots and you are like wow, check at that. Years later, you find yourself watching the rugby or soccer one evening, you have a piece of string in your hand, and you absent-mindedly tie knots. That is how we learn, it is the pull it back which is also hard, and then it is the automation process. Implementing that in what I do is not so easy, but that is what I do.

===*you got involved in the stock market as well, how were you introduced to this and by who*===

In 1982, I am 12years old, I had inherited some shares from my grandmother, and when I say some, I mean like 10 De Beers shares. It gets me interested, but they are not worth very much. My grandfather had been involved in the bucket industry in Durban in the 1920s; he was born in the 1800s. So he teaches me a whole lot about this and that gets my interest. I am reading the Sunday papers; I am reading Richard Glover who wrote in the Tribune. I would go to a stock market college although they charged thousands of rands. My thinking is I would rather buy shares than an expensive course. I would write letters to companies asking for their annual reports, they sent it to me, and for me this is mind blowing. You know I am a 16-year-old kid and they send me hundred pages. Then I write to every company and that just got me hugely interested. I am fascinated by how it works and fascinated by the fact that you can make money. Then there is the whole Bull Run up to 1987, and then there is the market crash. There was then the run in the 90s right into the '98 crash. It got me interested and then I received some very small inheritances, but inheritances which in retrospect the best thing I did, I bought shares with it. I bought Sasol at R22, I bought Pick 'n Pay although I subsequently sold them and bought Shoprite. It was just the fascination with me. The mistake I made perhaps was that I went and decided I wanted to do the trading thing and lost fortunes there. If I had gone and bought boring shares, it would be a lot of money today; fortunately, I kept my shares and the like. The whole way the thing worked, the whole process of companies, of listing, buying & selling; the psychology of it things like buy the rumor and sell the fact. You do not buy when the announcement happens because everyone has been buying ahead of the announcement anticipating how the market looks forward. It just absolutely fascinated me. I had always thought and this goes back into my attempt to get into journalism at Natal Technikon that it was not as hard as it looked, that we needed to get it to a lot more people. That is why I needed the column; I did not quite know how to do this as I said we did not have internet really in those days, but I wanted to do something around this sort of space and the stock market just fascinated me.

===*so was Sasol your first stock*===

No my very first stock was actually Didata, which I bought approximately 4 days before the crash of '87. I actually wanted to buy Datatec, but my stockbroker misheard and bought Didata. I bought them in my matric year and I had three jobs at the time so I had saved up about R160 or so. I bought them at splits adjusted at about 5 cents a share, but then the market crashed and I tried to sell them. I did not realize that the deal my grandfather had with the stockbroker was that my grandfather would pay for the costs of the purchases and not the sales. So I couldn't sell the Didata because the costs were more than the value of the shares so I left them. Then they did a ten for one split in about 1996 – 1997 and I forgot I owned them. I got a share certificate saying that you are the proud owner of however many Didata shares and I looked at the market and they were worth about R5.60 each and I paid adjusted about 5cents each. From there they went to R70.

===*what was your selection strategy the time you bought them*===

My strategy was simple, I mean make no mistake my strategy was not smart. My strategy was '87 computers are starting to come around and I had done some computer science at school, but very basic stuff. You not even doing machine coding, you are doing basic coding that is your coding language and the like. My father had a ZX 48k Spectrum so I was playing on that. Everyone used to say to me what am I going to go into and I would say computers, in truth, I flipped into finance. Back then, we did not realize that these days everyone is into computers and your cell phone is a computer, they surround us. Then this was like the exciting new space and I just knew I had to have a computer business and somehow I knew there was Didata and Datatec. I did not know what either of them did; I just wanted to buy one. And as I said I wanted Datatec, I don't know why, but I ended up with Didata. So there was no strong thought process beyond, "hey computers are exciting" and there were probably other stocks I could have bought that did better or worse. I do not know it was just luck then.

===*Do you think the internet has had any role in how long investors keep they stocks for nowadays? For example, I sometimes end up checking my portfolio daily and this sometimes leads to me selling the shares without following my strategy. I just do this because it is easy to do*==

Absolutely, because if we go back to '87 which is 27years ago, far enough back. I mean back in those days how did you get information, you did not. There was no radio shows, no magazines, there might have been the Financial Mail, I cannot remember. There was none of that sort of thing. What you did was that you bought the JSE handbook, which got updated every 6months and then you wrote to company secretaries and requested the annual reports and the like. So your information flow was incredible slow, when you copied information it was very old. Now we are getting bombarded and even now as we sit here there is stuff getting flung at my computer, my phone, my Ipad, everything. So information comes at us quicker and we respond quicker and we think we are in a better place. I am not sure we are, to your point I think we get pushed off into decisions. You do all the hard work, you buy the share, and I am going to leave it to my children. Then some single piece of information comes and it spooks you be it price movement or something. Back in the '80s we never saw that kind of information, the next day you would grab a newspaper and it would have a list of shares. You could then phone your broker and ask him why it moved and he would probably say he had no idea. The information was slow, we made slow decisions and I think slow decisions are better. Back to how we think there is a brilliant book out there called Thinking Fast & Slow. Our brain defaults to the quick thinking because it is easy. I give you $2 + 2 = 4$, I say to you 19 x 38 = mmm? So we default to the quick thinking rather than the slow thinking. The decision you spent time thinking about is invariably a better decision.

===*would you say you had a personal mentor at the time and if so, what came out of the relationship*===

No I didn't, but my grandfather thought me a lot. I suppose in a sense he was a mentor, I could phone him and ask him stuff. I am not dismissing him in the least; many times, he did not have the answers to what I was asking. He had been a jobber in the bucket shops, he knew a bit about the market. I never really had a mentor at any point in my career for me the internet became that in a sense and that was the beauty. In 1995, I got internet access and it was very, very rudimentary; it was dial up modems and it was incredibly slow. What I discovered out there was a world of other people on chat groups and bulletin boards who I could ask. There have been numerous people over the years that have my answered questions for me, and helped me move my knowledge forward. A single person, no; collectively it has been access to the internet which has been the most amazing thing ever.

===*just looking at the books I have read, I find that some of the successful traders went bust or got really close to it. Would you say you suffered the same experience*===

Oh, yes! When I was trading sort of 1995 to 2000, I think I destroyed three portfolios and by destroy I mean I took them down to zero or close to it. The point was in those days because of what you were trading which were either shares or options you could not go below zero. These days with CFDs and Futures, you can lose more than you start with so you put in R10000 and you could lose R20000. I bust out three times '95 and '99 both years inclusive I lost money in my trading space. My investing was paddling along I had some shares and they were doing ok. It was only in 2000 that I started to make some profit and a couple of things hit me; I read Reminiscence of a Stock Operator which is a brilliant book. I read Trading in the Zone by Mark Douglas. Sometimes you read a book very seldom and this is one of the examples where you read a book, a thousand lights go off your head, and suddenly you realize that you doing everything wrong. It is not a light switch moment, it is a process to follow, but the point is I made a profit from trading for the first time ever. I have never had a loss-making year since then and it was a slow grind. Now at least I knew what I needed to focus on and that was psychology. It has been a very, very long road for me to get to a point where I am confident enough to say, "I am trader". I still say it carefully because I am not going to make the mistake to say I am at the top. I am still learning and maybe I learn less than someone starting out, but there is still stuff to learn. A lot of what you are learning is about yourself, trading is psychology.

===*I am assuming that the losses might have been overwhelming at the time, what kept you going*===

I was doing very well in the publishing industry, so I had decent money and my wife had a job. We do not have kids and what did they call it those days, "DINKYs" (double income no kids). I did two things cleverly and one is I never put vast of money into the market. I cannot remember exactly how much it was, maybe of the three portfolios I blew out it was probably R60 000 – R80 000, maybe R90 000. It was big money, but it was not a killer amount. What kept me going is an interesting one because I meet a lot of traders who are struggling and not succeeding, the question from them is why do I carry on going? I will tell you why I kept on going, (a) the fascination, the love of the market and how it intersected with the internet. How those two completely democratised an entire industry and revolutionised investing or trading for the person in the street like it had never been before. (b) It was just a single-minded belief when I looked at it, I could do this. I did not know how, but I knew I could. It is the one thing that my mother always instilled in me, she used to say to me; Simon you can do anything you want. Not because I am special, although I believed that is what she was saying, but because if you put your mind to it, we can do astounding things. Can we walk on water; no! However, if we are single minded about something and we put our heads down, just focus and do. When problems come just bat them aside and realize that your journey is not a straight line from A-B. Your journey is a zigzag line, you are going to go in circles for ages, and that is part of the mess. The determination is the one thing I have and as I said, my mother taught me that. When I put my mind to it there is a single-minded determination and belief that problems are just things I have not solved yet; I do not know how, but I will solve them. There is no unique problem, any problem that I come up against, I am not the first person to come up against that problem which means there is a solution and I just have to find it.

===*that makes plenty of sense. Would it be correct to view trading as a business? I am thinking now in a sense where you have to get up, dress up and go to work and at the end of each month take inventory*===

Yes, you are 100% spot on. To your comment this morning when you arrived here, you said I am not in a suit, so I wear a suit when I am on TV and doing presentations. Trading is a business, I get dressed in the morning, I put socks and shoes on, and I come and sit in my office. It is a business from a mind perspective and you need to treat it like a business. Do not sit here in your pyjamas with yesterday's coffee lying around and stuff like that. Also from a practical perspective, I mean what is a losing trade; it is the cost of doing business. If you have a hotdog stand, the costs of doing business is buying inventories, buying hotdogs, rolls, tomato sauce and marketing. As a trader, you have costs of doing business, internet, software, brokerage fees, losing trades and you have to view it as a business; that is the right perspective. When you view it as I am trying to beat the market that I am trying to show the market how great I am, when you view it as I am trying to make vast amount of money, then you are in the wrong mind shift. You need to be in the mind shift and like any other business, there is process and you just follow process. Sometimes process makes money, sometimes it does not, but on a balance over all process will make you money. You could pick the wrong process, but the single most important part is process.

===*do you think it's better to starting with investing and later progress into trading*===

Yes, but people do it the other way around. They start with trading; why? Because you have R5000, R10 000 or R100 000 and you look at this and say, "Man, this investing thing is slow." So you go into trading where you have got derivates and gearing. You want to be a neurosurgeon at your first day in varsity and they give you a patient, sculpt and say fix the brain; no, the first day they show you pictures and teach you Latin. The point with investing is it is a lot more forgiving and when I mean investing I do not mean go and buy a smallcap stock and hope it will recover, go buy a boring blue chip stock when it is cheap. It gives you space, it is more forgiving if you make errors. It is going to create wealth overtime and I mean heck buy an ETF. It gives you that process of getting into the market, the learning curve and the like. The problem is we are in a hurry, now we say this generation is the fastest with all our WhatsApp, instant messaging, but every generation has had that, it has been different. My grandfather born in 1896 in Durban, it was horses and tracks. He talks about the first time he saw a motorcar and he thought it was the silliest thing he had ever seen. It was noisy, dirty, and smelly. For him that was radical technology and now for us it is WhatsApp and mobile phones, for our kids it will be who knows what? Going into investing taking it cautiously and realizing that your single biggest asset you have is time. You lose money, you can go and earn it back, you lose time, and it is gone. So what do we do when we start, we go into the risky space and lose money, but we do not only lose money; we lose time perhaps even worse we get discouraged and we exit entirely. If we go and say let us use this time in our favor. I speak to a lot of school children mostly in their 20s and I say forget about the conventional wisdom that says you are in your 20s you can take high risks. What about the fact that you are in your 20s and have four decades of market ahead of you; use that four decades, do not lose a single day, start with investing.

===*earlier on you mentioned that you were trading intraday sitting in front of the screen quite a lot. When did you decide to make trading a full time career*===

I was trading warrants and the date would have been late 2004, I am designing a couple of trading systems one of them my lazy trading system, although they would have been adapted in the 10years subsequent. I was trading warrants end of day basis and I discovered this thing called the ALSI – Futures and I decide to trade the ALSI – Futures. I find it the most amazingly simple thing in the world because all I do is I watch the price; I do not care about the news flow. I started to trade ALSI Index Futures in a 15-minute chart and I do it for about a year and a half and I make good money off it. I am clever enough that when I make money I am off buying boring shares, paying cash for a car and a second hand car add to that. What I realized essentially is that I have an 8-5 job except it is actually 8-8 because there would be admin and that it is momentously boring, just killingly boring. This is not what I wanted to spend the rest of my life doing, yes the money is great do not get me wrong. At that point I am in my mid-30s and if you tell that me I am doing this for the next 30years, the idea of it kills me with dread. I stopped it. I do not recall when, but when I woke up one day and I was like nope, not doing that anymore. That is when I started focusing on the website and we dominated our niche. And also the markets moved away from warrants, the market moved into single stock futures, index futures and I kind of got a little left behind. That is in 2006 and around when Standard Bank called and it happened to be in good timing.

===*Simon, you later sold SA Warrants, was that always part of the plan*===

Look every business I start, the plan is to sell it. The mistake we often make when we start businesses is that as the founder we put ourselves too much in the business. In other words what I am saying is can you sell the business without you as an individual. The problem with SA Warrants is that it was very hard to sell it without me. There were parts we could sell without me, the subscription service we sold, the warmap we sold, but the commentary and the teaching was not SA Warrants that was actually Simon Brown. That is a lesson I learnt in my first business and I just kept on repeating it. The mistake that we make where the business is not XYZ business, the business is the individual more than anything else. This business I just started JustOneLap I did very differently. I outsourced a lot of the stuff. I mean can I code HTML website. Yes, but are there expects out there, yes. Same with images, editing I got experts to do it. I am still in a position where I think I am too central to the business, but less so. It is easier in this situation with JustOneLap to extract me out and have a business that is viable going forward without me. It is going to be hard because there is a lot of linkage between the two, but a lot less so than the case with SA Warrants.

===*when you spoke about the magazine earlier on, it sounded like you had partners, what's your view on partnership in a sense that is it something that one should consider or stay away from*===

Both, I have had bad examples with partners and I have had good examples with partners. I will tell you what partners bring which is really good; they bring skill sets which you might not have. They also bring a counter to you so if you go barreling off someone can say hang on pause, why are you doing that and what is happening there. So they are really useful in that sense, people to bounce ideas off and the like. Finding that partner I suspect is immensely difficult and probably large amount of luck in the process and on balance of probability, I would probably say partners are good. If you however get the wrong partner, it can be very destructive. So I suppose the point is when you start a partnership, design a way to unwind the partnership. In other words, when you draw up that initial contract about being partners and have processes to dissolve the process if it does not work. There is a chance that it will not work, if it does not, you need to be able to dissolve it without killing the business and everything else in the process.

===*interesting approach to that. Working at Standard Online Share Trading would you say being in an environment where other traders surrounded you helped you in your own trading*===

Not with my trading, a lot of them were jobbers. Online Share Trading was a non-advisory so there were traders on the floor particularly in Forex. They were on the far side and they were doing a lot of client orders rather than personal trading. What I did like, it was the first time apart from a year or so at Ster-Kinekor where I worked in a corporate environment. What I liked was having colleagues and it goes to my point about partners, people to bounce ideas off; that was absolutely great. Someone to go and have coffee with, currently I have coffee with my cat. The problem off course is that sometimes too many cooks spoil the broth type of scenario. It is a very, very fine balancing line, there was the global financial crisis our market peaked March 2008, and we saw a financial crisis unseen in our lives. Maybe worse than the 1930s global crisis, but certainly in our lifetime never witnessed, that was a learning experience. That was an experience of just do not panic, there is no upside to panic.

===*talking about market crashes, you were already involved a bit in the stock market during the crash of '87. I am assuming now that was still way in the early days for you. How was it and did you panic*===

Yes, yes. I got home from school, I do not remember the time, but I would have turned on the wireless. The crash was so bad it actually made the news and I hear there is a crash and off course, I panicked. The crash happened on a Tuesday and I had bought my Didata shares the preceding Thursday. So I try and phone my stock broker and off course the phones are just engaged. Eventually I get through to my stockbroker and he realises it is me and he just put the phone down. And in truth, I wasn't losing real money was I, I had a R100 or R200 in the market and he had clients with millions of rands. I absolutely panicked and when I got hold of him a while later and tried to sell I realized the problem where I had to pay the fees and I could not afford the fees. It taught me many things and up to that point, everything looked lovely and I had not heard these rumblings about crashes coming. These days with internet, you get these every minute of every day. Suddenly what looked rosy could turn on a dire, the bigger lesson is that things recovered and the market recovered within 2years. When I was buying Sasol shares in about '93 – 94, it was a case of they had significantly recovered. It was really an understanding that you can buy these and sort of hold on to them and that things will horrible go wrong at some point; overtime it will come back. Then there was the emerging market crisis of '98 and it's weird. So my first one is '87 and I panicked. The 1998 crash happened and I did it all wrong I sold at the bottom and bought at the top, but I did not panic at least. The 2000 Dot-com burst I kind of knew what was happening and my quality stuff I hung onto, but I also hung on to some really bad stuff I shouldn't have. The crisis of '08 I did perfectly well in some sense, I did not panic, and I started buying when there was blood on the floor. It's really weird it's almost the sense of I am ready for the next market crisis and let's be honest there has been 87, 97, 01, 07; I have gone through four of them. Now I think the next one I will probably do ok. It comes back to the point that you learn slowly hey, this is a 27-year process since the crash of '87 to now and I am like bring it on. It has taken a long time to get here.

===*you have also co-founded Tickertalk and that is something I do not hear you talk about, can you enlightened what that is all about*===

Tickertalk was a business I started with three partners Stuart Thompson, Mike Melville and a technology partner Virtual Works. We did this late 2009, the idea was quite simply, Facebook for investors. It did not work for a couple of reasons, maybe because we are ahead of our time, but that is probably stroking our ego. Our tech was not very good; there were functionality issues with the website; user interface was not very good and we could not get the traction we really needed. It kind of occasional flirted to deceive; it looked like it could be something and then fall back. Then I think it got superseded by the technology such as Twitter and I think we have been taken over to a fair degree by other techs. We are now in a lengthy process of actually selling it. It will be a sale or bring on a partner and then re-launch it. In my heart of hearts, I think it was a brilliant idea poorly executed and I think that is one of my core things. Business ideas, I do not think they are the scarcity; there are a lot of business ideas out there. I remember sitting down with people I worked with because they hated their jobs; well I said fine, we sat down and drew a list of 100 businesses. It is not about the idea; it is about the execution and Tickertalk I think we executed poorly.

===earlier on you also mentioned something about putting time in a business. Could this perhaps be an example===

There are negotiations happening with Tickertalk I am not sure where it is going to end up and my biggest problem now is that I work 12-hour days and I do not have any more hours left in my days. It is always the case that the most passive and simplest of businesses need time unless you go buy shares, I own Shoprite shares. I mean there is 50 000 Shoprite people out there today working to make me a profit that is true passive, but if you own a business directly, man there is always work.

===*The name JustOneLap, does it hold any significance to you* ===

There are two things; firstly, you do not need your website to be descriptive. The biggest seller of books in the world is Amazon.com and not Books.com and the biggest job placement website in the world is not Jobs.com, it's Monster.com, so I got that. If you call yourself Books.com, you narrow yourself and I discovered that with SA Warrants, we were too narrow with that. I wanted a generic name and JustOneLap was quite simple; we get Just One Lap at life do not mess it up. Now for me I focus on money, but off course that includes as I mentioned already relationships, careers, health, and the like. If you are in a rut, then get out of it. If you do not like where you are right now in your life and if you are not actively working to change it, you will still be there in 5years time! Do not wait for some magic thing to happen unexpectedly like winning the Lotto or something. If you are not doing something about it, it is not going to change. We get Just One Lap, if you are not happy then do something about it.

===*now when you start these businesses what kind of*

expectations do you have at the start in terms of the response? Most of us will normally have negative thoughts, which can eventually be a hindering factor===

When I started SA Warrants I had not expectations, it was just a hobby. Part of the trick was that I was getting so many questions around warrants via email and it was taking too many hours of my days, so I thought I will start the website and when people ask questions, I will just throw it into the website. If I look at JustOneLap, when you start businesses, they are going to be slower and harder than you thought. If you start a business and your aim is to have a billion users like Facebook, you are crazy. When you start a business, have a high road, low road and a middle road; in other words, whether that is revenue, users, or anything like that. My rule of thumb is whatever your high road is, cut it in half; that number that you think, half it and then from there is a middle road and a low road. If the low road is still profitable and makes financial sense then you have a business you can try. With JustOneLap I am still on the middle road and I would love to say I am on the high road, but in truth the growth and users are at the middle road. If I sat down and said my target with JustOneLap is a million users, I will be deluding myself.

===the slogan "Know your money, Grow you money", let me rather stick to myself here and say I struggled with that when I started working, especially the credit side of things. Would you say

you had a similar experience===

Look I have gone through all the mistakes. I have had debt, I have taken loans I should not have and I have bought things on credit I shouldn't have and the like. I have managed my money poorly and I have had no money at one point. I have gone to the ATM, punched in my secret code and the ATM said nope, you don't have anything here anymore. And off course I would accuse the ATM of stealing my money. It's about that taking responsibility, it's part of the whole JustOneLap and if you are not taking responsibility for your life whichever part it maybe, the question then is who is. I used to use an analogy of who is driving your bus. You are definitely on a bus and if you are not driving it, then someone else is. If they are driving it then it might seem all comfortable sitting at the back because you do not have to worry about driving, but the truth is then where are you going? You are going to where the driver wants to go, I mean who are they and where do they want to go and have they been drinking and all those sort of questions. So it is really about taking responsibility. The "Know your money, Grow you money" tries to say this is not rocket science. The problem is I experienced it, you experienced it and everyone out there, who teaches us about money; no one. It is not our parents, because they were not taught about it and I am not dissing our parents, they were simply not taught about money. It is not our grandparents, not our teachers, it is not our governments, and they are the worst. I mean most governments on this planet including America; if you run a balance sheet on them, they are technically bankrupt and they borrow more than they can get in. So who is teaching us about money, short answer, you have to do it yourself. It is not rocket science, it goes back to spend less than you earn. I am now in a situation where I have credit cards; I use two of them, one for work and the other for personal use. I have no debt, I buy second hand cars and I pay cash for them. I have no store card and I have not had a store card in a decade. I have a home loan only because my money does better in the stock market than the cost of the home loan. I have a positive balance sheet and most people do not even know what their balance sheet is.

===*there is one video I like on your website about paying your home loan in 7years, is that something you have done yourself*===

The reason I picked 7 years is because the average person in South Africa buys a house every 7years; they sell the one and they are constantly upgrading. The problem is we call a house an asset, now there is a huge debate around this and we could spend an hour talking about it. I do not believe your home is an asset; in fact I have come to believe recently that you are better off renting from a financial perspective than buying. You buy a house for R500 000 and you pay R2 000 000 on it, of which R1 500 000 is interest. You are better off putting that R1 500 000 into the stock market and investing it. The first house I bought was in 1998, which was at the bottom of the property market so I got it cheap, but I got it at crazy interest rates. I sold it in 2007 and at that point, I had not paid off the bond. In fact, I had re-bonded it; I had gone into one of those classic mistakes. I partly re-bonded to improve the house, but I also partly re-bonded and I will be honest, I do not know where the other money went. Then I came to Joburg, I was in a situation where I could afford to buy the house because I managed to sell my house in KZN for a couple of hundred thousand extra. Now I am not going to buy a fancy expensive house, I cannot see the point of that. I decided to take the bond because I would rather take that cash and put it in the stock market. The math is simple take a long return on the stock market and by long term, I am talking decades. The stock market return including dividends is higher than the average prime rate in the South African economy. In other words, your prime rate is 10% and stock market return is 15%, you are better off putting that money in the stock market than paying your bond massively quickly. Now I am very, very careful giving that advice to people for a bunch of reasons. Firstly, you have to have the discipline to leave that money in the stock market when it crashes. Secondly, you have to able to afford the bond payments and include losing your job; do you have 6 – 12 months bond payments while you find a new job etcetera. The biggest problem with buying a house is the costs; it is hugely expensive. Upfront there are transfer fees, maintenance cost and there are agent fees when you sell, property is very expensive. When I finally leave Joburg one day, will I sell the house, yes, because I do not like tenants! A year ago, I would have said to you I would buy another house, now I am not so sure, to me the math says rent.

===traders talk of risk management especially about how much capital you are prepared to lose per trade. When starting a company, do you have something similar in place===

A lot of my companies that I have started, I really started with very small amounts. Many of them have costs me less than a R1000 to start. I mean with SA Warrants it was R400 for server hosting and the domain registration that was my costs the first year. Most of my businesses I start with tiny overheads, I work from home. I looked at the numbers this year about getting a nice decent office in Melrose, Rosebank, it's convenient because it's 5minutes from the Gautrain. It is right by the JSE, Business Day TV and Standard Bank, which are a few of my business clients, but it is the costs. This office does not cost me anything. I try to start them very cheap and as I have said with JOL, I have done some differences. I brought in expects to design the website and other things, but certainly they were costs I could cover well within my savings. I would never start a business that runs the risk of bankrupting me and some people may say that I will never be focused enough, it depends on the individual. Personally, I can focus without the fear of getting bankrupt. I have spent 44years getting to this point I do not think there is anything out there and it is a good position. I could retire, my quality of life would go down; I would have to drink wine out of a box rather than out of a bottle. I do not think any business or anything is worth risking that position. Maybe it is just me being old.

===*I listened to you present a number of times and two things stood out for me:*

- *"We are brought up with the core belief that to succeed in life we need to work hard" – Looking at your kind of work, it's fairly simply compared to taking a shovel and digging a trench*
- *"Discipline"*

Do you think these two apply in other spheres of our lives as well===

Look, I get your point on the working; to me the working hard is knowledge work. Sometimes I work 12-hour days and by the end of the day, my head hurts. I mean is it good old-fashioned working hard my father used to do as a 17-year-old boy digging trenches, not even close. It goes to the point that we are brainwashed to believe, particularly around the corporate; you sell yourself to a corporate and you put 16hours a day. Do they really care about you, maybe not! There are ways in a sense when we can almost say work smart rather than hard. I do six jobs, I work hard and I have 6 different bosses who I do work for, then off course 6 different bosses I get to invoice every month which is the plus side of it. It is about working hard stream lining and the like. At this point, in the year, I am tired, it is the end of September and I am thinking to myself that I need to work less hard next year. It is not just the hard work that is going to get success; it is discipline and particularly in the trading space. We think that trading is going to be the hardest thing ever, when you get to the point of successful trading it takes me less than half an hour a week. Discipline, without discipline what are we? We would randomly run around screaming our heads off if we do not have discipline. We obey the rules of culture, norm and of the country we are in; but also discipline to see things through. Things are going to get tough in any business you need that discipline to see it through. You need that discipline to pivot where you have to and make changes when you need to. It is not army level discipline, but the discipline to keep our promises, discipline to do what we say when we say type of scenario.

===*looking at your career now, what is the one thing you would say you learnt and has stood out for you over time*===

That luck plays an unordinary role in how things happen and sometimes it might be bad luck. I will give you a good example, I mentioned that SA Warrant was doing ok, and I made the front page of the Business Times. The back-story to that is, Jeremy Thomas contacted me and he wanted to do a story, I sent him some stuff. He had a photographer in Durban, which he sent to my house to take a photograph of me. My office was literally a circle, it was an old hut and at that point I had very long hair. I am sitting in a crazy bright yellow New York taxi t-shirt and the photographer takes a crazy picture of me holding my laptop up. He sent it to Johannesburg and in Johannesburg, they said it's a great photo and a great story. That was just luck, luck that there was a photographer, luck that he did not just take a boring photograph; so many angles of luck. From that, SA Warrant became huge, I became known and everything follows from that. In truth there has been bunches of good and bad luck in my life, if you remove any one of them from the equation, I am still doing well. I am just not sitting right where I am now, but luck is there. You pitching for some work and your main competitors have a typo and they add an extra zero to their bid price, so you win it. You were not cheaper than they were, it was just luck. Luck is difficult because we cannot plan for it, but when it comes along, grab it with both hands. Be honest, do not say that was me, accept that this was just luck. Understand that sometimes that there is bad luck, do no hate the world, just put your head down, and work for it.

===*what would you say you enjoy the most these days, you have mentioned that you have six bosses*===

What I love the most about my work is two things: I wake up early 5 o'clock or so and I look at my calendar and sometimes it is packed. Nearly every day I look at the things in that calendar and I know it is going to be fun. It is going to be learning, it is going to be teaching, going to Cape Town or Durban for presentations. It is just going to be about doing stuff I am passionate about, I love the stock market and I love teaching people about the stock market. The days are sometimes exhausting; I look at it and think this is going to be a fun day and that is what drives me. I have always promised myself that if I am not enjoying what I do, I will stop doing it; mostly I have kept to that promise. Every year I look at my six bosses and say which one of you are not fun anymore. The years since I have left Standard Bank, I have cancelled a number of contracts. I have gone to folks and said I do not want to renew this contract next year because it just does not work for me; we get too hooked into it. We get just one lap at life, if we are not having fun at that lap, change it.

===annual events that happen in the industry, what would you advise people to attend===

Keep it simple; also, it depends where you are. If you are in the major centers, you will find the big stockbrokers Standard Online Share in particular and there are others as well, the JSE also does events. Do not be in a hurry; go to the basic one, introduction to investing. Look around online you will find JustOneLap all over the place, you will find a ton of content out there, keep it simple. Start at the beginning start at A, don't jump at W and think you will get to Z by the weekend.

===Simon what is your typical day like, starting from early in the morning===

Friday is a bad day because Friday is a half day. I work in the morning, I record a TV show at lunchtime, and my afternoon is hugely free. My weekdays I am up early 05:00 to 05:30 and I have coffee or juice, not a breakfast fan. Typically, at my desk by 07:30 showered, shaved and ready to rock and roll. Check my trading system and see if there is anything there. Check my emails; check my social media for both the incoming and outgoing. My first engagements of the day are usually not before 08:30. It will be meetings and stuff like that; I am not necessarily watching the market all the time. My day is then going to be teaching stuff, webcasts and it might be one on ones. Also then, planning future events, taking events I did today, compiling videos, rendering, uploading, promoting and marketing. Writing more content cause there is always content for the website, there is content for Finweek, there's interviews I am doing. I have TV shows I record Tuesday and Wednesday evenings. Then if I have presentations, sort of 16:00 get showered and suited up and head off to the venue. It is not massively structured except that the core theme is I am teaching, I am creating content and I am getting it on the internet. I am getting out there and I am seeing what the internet is sending to me that's in terms of what users are saying and what things are people talking about. Also looking if there is an angle, I can use to teach or add to it.

----------------------------END----------------------------

As I drove through the streets of Johannesburg to interview Simon, a number of thoughts made their way to my mind. The first one was about when I first saw him presenting at a Standard Bank Online Share Trading (OST) seminar in Cape Town. He spoke so passionately about investing and trading. I recall him saying most people do not succeed in trading and that some had a better chance of making money working at MacDonalds. Instead of listening to what was being said and digesting it in a proper manner, I kept on thinking I am not most people and later paid the lesson of not looking for similarities in what he had to say.

Second thought that came in my mind was what I could call the first lesson I learnt before the interview. I had no doubt in my mind that Simon was a successful man and as my mind would have it, I pictured this huge mansion, 4 garage doors, massive pool and an SUV parked in the yard. I had seen the gent on local television shows; I had followed his trading and investment performance on social networks. To me it was all justified that he should have a 3-storey house. As I was thinking about this, I noticed my navigator indicated that I am just less than 2km from his house and there was no sign of mansions nearby. I continued driving until I was right outside his house and as soon as he came out to meet me the thought of a mansion quickly vanished. I currently have a bonded house and there is part of me that wanted to upgrade to something more expensive. Here was a man who could well afford something much more than I could and later he makes an example about getting a new office; he also asks what would be the point of it. I came inside a cosy home with standard furnishing, just the kind I would like one day when I finally retire in some village. Later in the interview, he explains that his house if fully paid and does not really see the need to buy another.

Before the interview starts, we chat about a number of things, particularly how I came about writing this book. As I explained to him, I went as far as discussing how we now pay people to do everything for us such that we miss out on some of life's valuable lessons. The lessons may not necessarily bring any financial gain, but to a certain degree, they bring a sense of achievement. He quickly mentioned how he had an old big tree at the corner of his backyard and wanted to cut it down. He mentioned that he could have hired someone to cut it down, but decided to do it himself. He said he felt so good after cutting it down and now every time he use the logs to start a fire he feels that sense of achievement.

Now by the time the interview began, Simon knew exactly what I wanted, from the first 10 -20minutes he gave me all the information I needed from him after the first question. I was worried that I would not have any more questions to ask. He mentions that at his core he is nothing fancy, but a teacher and it is something he is passionate about it. I soon learnt that he had to work his way from a young age when he struggled with speech impediment and that did not get him down. I recall how I struggled in school when it came to making speeches or doing any kind of public talking. I would totally freak out and a lot of stuttering would follow this; to this very day, I struggle with it. As the interview starts, I notice that Simon has his whole life story in his head and he is able to recall a number of things well without any struggle. At some of these, I could see the expression on his face and they meant something to him. He later tells me that when he completed matric he was obliged to do national service or continue studying, he makes his first decisive choice right there that there is no way he would go and do national service. Again later, he says, *"I have always promised myself that if I am not enjoying what I do I will stop doing it."* What I am getting though is that this was not always easy for him; the choices came with consequences, whenever things were not going well, he would go back to restaurants to find work. What was more interesting was how he was rejected by a varsity because he failed matric, later admitted to studied film and video; as he says this he has a smile on his face. Now I know of a few people that had the same experience when applying at varsity, not being able to study what they wanted because of their results. I for one wanted to study quantity survey, but because the course had been fully enrolled for that year; I was forced to study anything with survey, and ended up studying engineering survey. Does this mean I would have made a better quantity surveyor, maybe not? Simon mentions that they tried to launch an extreme sports magazine and it did not work. He goes on to say that, it is possible that it was too early, and the market was not ready for such at the time. He also says that there is no bad business, but the execution of the idea is important. After launching a successful website SA Warrants, he goes into another business venture Tickertalk, this also does not work well for him. On his current business JustOneLap he tells us that he did a lot of things differently, he outsourced most of the design work. He is also quick to say that he could have done this himself, but thought he must just get the right kind of people in this time around. A few things I learnt from this: When I was doing this interview, I happened to launch a company called Mzantsi Hitchers, which was supposed to be a lift sharing service and carpooling. I knew that many people could find this service very useful, but my execution was not necessarily up to standard. Firstly, I hired the wrong people from the start thinking I could manage to cut costs. Secondly, the market I was targeting was not ready for this. A quick example would have been launching a cell phone service in the most remote part of Africa in 1995. The intention was a good one, people needed to establish some kind of communication. However, would they have found the service worthwhile when they did not even have electricity? Simon also shares with me how what he had learnt in film and video is helping him with his current work editing videos. He did not just learn something and forget about it once he moved on; again, this comes up when he speaks of how people learn. He makes an example of tying a knot; something simple, how we are able retrieve this information if we reach deep into our memory bank. What I also find interesting is that he went from someone who struggled to read to having a library of 5000 books. Yes, this might not make sense, but one can clearly see what the books have done for him. I struggle a lot with reading and will occasionally pick up a book or two. He wanted to be a financial journalist, and he has managed to do just that, without a tertiary degree in that field. One of the clear indications I pick up is that if we really want something in life, we will get it; if we can just focus all our strength into achieving it. He also admits that sometimes we fall into things and do not necessarily have a plan for everything

Another lesson I pick up from Simon is that we sometimes fall into stuff and when this happens, it could have all kinds of positive implications that come with it. When I started working on this book, I knew I wanted it to changes someone else life one day and before it did that, it changed my life. I think the most important thing that dawned for me was that I should keep an open mind. Opportunities will come my way, I just need to keep record of I what I am truly interested in.

IGOR MARINKOVIC OF TRADING WSDOMS

INTRODUCTION: I attended a seminar about 4 years ago and the presenter spoke about an investor up in the capital city that traded the stock market. He went to speak of how this investor managed to build a property portfolio just north of 40; this investor was about 38 years at the time. Around about then, I had invested in property myself and I was just learning about tenant problems, body corporate, I could go on. I had not grasped the gent's name from the presentation, but through navigating the social networks, I came across Igor.

===*this is a story that really got my attention that I went out on social networks searching for this investor. I found him on Twitter eventually. Igor, can you give a bit of background as in where were you born and studied*===

I was born in 1973 in a country known at that stage as Yugoslavia, but during the 90s, there was a very ugly civil war there. The country was split into three different countries and the part that I am from is called Serbia. If you watch local soccer, the coach of Orlando Pirates right now Vladimir Vermezovic, is from Serbia as well. My parents raised me, my mother was a professor at a technikon and my father was manager at the bank. I attend primary and secondary school in my city which is really a small city with about 90 000 people. When I went to university, I went to the biggest city which had about 400 000 people and I studied electronic engineering, I got an honours and master's degree in that. In the 2000, I came to South Africa as I had a job offer from a company, which went into provisional liquidation. I found it on the net, I sent them my CV, and they accepted it. So I moved to South Africa on the 22 August 2000 just a few days after I got married.

===*in terms of studying would you say that electrical engineering was always your passion*===

I guess as a kid I have always had that engineering mind set and I did not think about too many things. I liked mathematics from the beginning, even in primary and secondary school I went to intra-city and intra-school competitions. So I decided to study electrical engineering, I liked that, I liked to make small circuit boards while I was in high school as well, so that was my first choice.

Second choice would have definitely been B.Comm or Economic Science because I really liked what my dad did in terms managing the local bank. I really liked spending my holidays at his office looking at how he was dealing with people and what kind of things he did. That would have been my second option, but unfortunately the civil war just broke and with electrical engineering you could postpone going into the army and with economic science you could not. If I had studied, economic science I would probably never ended up in South Africa.

===*eventually you ended up doing exactly that, economics*===

Yes, somehow, all the cubes ended up falling into place and the dots connected.

===*investing, was that also part of the dream or you just*

stumbled on it===

To be honest at that stage, Yugoslavia was a communist country. There was no investment; the government owned your flat, all companies only the exception of small shops selling ice cream that was privately owned. That was still 1990 for sure and from 1990 to 2000, the transition started, but unfortunately, we sat at that stage with massive inflation and the biggest in the world. It was war and it was very ugly. Somehow, in that period, the stock market was open, but I completely missed it and I did not know about it. So coming here in South Africa in 2000, I had no idea about investing at all. I came to work as an engineer as many people say or as Robert Kiyosaki says, "go to school, get good grades, and find a job and work"; that was my idea. Starting to think about it, I came wanting to study MBA and continue with my education. Then I stumbled across Robert Kiyosaki's Rich Dad, Poor Dad and that book opened my mind for sure. I bought the book at Exclusive Books and I read it throughout the night. From that moment, I forgot about doing my MBA and I started thinking about investing. That book really opened my mind, maybe for somebody else it is too simple, but coming from the communist background it was an amazing book.

===still with your engineering work, did you ever think of having your own company one day or that thought never crossed

your mind===

The problem with the field I specialise in is that to open a company you must have quite an immense background. We are designing integrated circuits and all of them, are manufactured in China. Our process of designing new integrated circuits lasts for probably 6 months and that includes a team of 5 or 10 engineers. There is only one company South Africa that does that and it is located in Paarl, in Cape Town. It is a big investment outline in the beginning to have something like that. I never really dreamt about that, but what happened for me to start investing in property is that some friend of ours we met in church also from Serbia currently with a massive property portfolio worth millions of rands coming every month through rent. He came to South Africa 1974, he did not speak English, and he did not know how to do anything. He started with laying bricks on a construction site, started thinking about building one small-scale house, and then sells it. He then noticed that the houses that he sold 3 – 4 years earlier were selling at 2-3 times the price they were when he sold them. He started building a few houses but kept one or two for himself and today he does not build any new property, he just rents or buys a new one. So that's how I got the idea about property investment. I stumbled across that guy and told myself that if he can do it, nothing is stopping me from doing it.

===*so is it only property that you invest in or do you have other investments*===

Yes, only property; mainly units that are for rental purposes. It is mostly in the CBD areas like Sunnyside, Hillbrow, Berea and Yeoville in Jo'burg. The thinking is that the demand in those areas is massive while the supply is small. In the area where I stay, they can easily go and build another block next door with 500 units and obviously affecting your rental. In areas like Sunnyside, it is a project, first you do not have space and secondly the demand for the people who want to stay there is amazing.

===*when you started, did you have some kind of direction that this is going to be your investment style? For example in my case, I heard that property is a good investment and I bought the first thing I came across. I totally had no direction, strategy in place. Did you perhaps do little more research*===

The first thing I came across was just a real estate magazine that had a list of properties for sale. This was back in 2005 when I bought my first property I noticed property prices were appreciating in some areas except Sunnyside, which was pretty much stable at that stage. I wanted to find out why property prices in one area a few kilometres away were going up while in Sunnyside they were stable. So I started investigating and found that someone selling a unit on Private Property. I went there and you would not believe the kind of arguments I had with my friends, saying I should not invest in Sunnyside. They were saying there is crime; people will rob you, rape or kill you. Then I said wait, it is impossible to say that every person in Sunnyside is a criminal. So the first time my wife and I went there we left everything at home and just took one cell phone and no one even noticed us. Yes, most of the people are black and I am white, sorry if that sounds racist, but it was like that and even today, it is still like that. The person who was selling the property was from Vanderbilpark and his kids stayed there because they were studying in Pretoria. I spoke to him and he said he has never had a problem, so we bought the property and that was my first property. The only thing I wanted was that the property should be just breakeven when I sell it or a little bit less because at that stage, my wife and I were still working, the salaries were still low. We had just bought our first property, putting in some furniture; remember we came to South Africa with nothing only clothes in our bags. I looked for a property where if I had to pay in, it would be a little bit extra every month. Therefore, I would keep it minimal, about R200 – R300 and not more; that was basically the idea at the beginning. Obviously, we were scared to death with the first property; we were thinking we had made a mistake. Then off course came the 2nd, 3rd, 4th, 5th and you do not even count afterwards.

===*with the rental, do you have agents running them for you*===

At the beginning, I had agents on one or two flats, but in the end, you end up chasing the rental agency to pay you your money instead of the tenant and they charge you 10%. Usually everybody says they will transfer the money by the 7th of each month, by the 10th you call them and they do not even know who you are. I decided against that, although I have an agency for two small block buildings I have in Jo'burg. The reason for that it is simply too cost effect for me to go there each time and do it myself, but here in Pretoria I do it myself.

===*look, I understand your selection strategy very well, but was the some kind of price you were looking at? An example would be looking at a specific range of 200 – 300k*===

Well at the start, I was buying anything I could get my hands on. At that stage, property prices were going up quite quickly. A two bedroom flat would go from R250 000 to R400 000 and I stopped buying then because it was too expensive. For example I bought the first property for R250 000 and a year later the price was R400 000 and the rent had increased a little. After that, I stayed with 10 places for about 2-3years and when the interest rates went up in 2008 that is when I was buying the big chunk of property. I just went to auctions and most of those flats I have never seen before I bought them, I only saw them when they were being registered in my name. I sat at the auction and if property bids were at R250 000 and I knew I would get R4500 rental out of it, I would buy it. Now I am getting sick and tired of sectional titles because you have a body corporate, people who do not pay the levies or they are struggling to pay the levies. What sometimes happens in such cases is they raise a special levy, which affects the people that are paying. So now, I look for small buildings in the Jo'burg CBD with maybe 6 or 10 flats.

===*I imagine that you have to spend some time renovating some of them*===

It all depends, most of the time I just paint them and put new tiles, that is mostly the case, I do not do any structural changes because then you need municipal approval and things like that. I know people that buy the building with about 6 flats, 3bedroom flats; they apply to the municipality and covert it to 18 to 20 bachelor flats putting in a new bathroom and stuff. Then again, that is a lot of capital at the beginning. So for I now I like to keep the building as it is, make money from it and as the time progresses, I will slowly make changes. You know when you see a building the first time it is one thing and then another after you have spent some time working on it.

===*I am starting to understand the pros of your investment style, what are the cons. You mentioned earlier on about the body corporate*===

The buildings in those areas are old and for quite some time were never maintained properly. In some areas, the lifts are not working and to upgrade the lift costs you a few million rands, which is ridiculous and to close the lift you must again pay a fee. Then again, that is just part of the cost of running a business. Currently I pay 2-3 special levies a month with my portfolio, which goes from R300 – R1000; and that is quite steep. I feel like some reputable companies like Trafalgar though run some buildings and they are doing their best, for example in the Pretoria area, they are putting up water meters now in each flat. There are many people putting in 20 people in a two bedroomed flat causing a slum kind of a scenario. So now, everyone gets to pay equally and fairly. There are many cons, but they are not an exception in any business.

===*Do you buy these properties for long term or short-term purpose*===

It is for long term and passive income. I have never sold a single property in my life and I do not think I will ever sell any. Every property we buy, we think of buying it for the kids as it generates a very nice cash flow each month and the rent just keeps going up.

===*Do you buy the properties cash*===

No, they are all bank financed.

===*How do you find that, is it easily accessible*===

These days it's very difficult, 2-3 years ago it was easy; but with things like the National Credit Act, being self-employed and buying the property in a trust it's getting difficult to get finance through the bank. For the small buildings that I buy in the CBD of Jo'burg there's a company called TUFH (Trust for Urban Housing Finance). They do not look at your income or salary; they just look at the building and how much it is worth, how much income you can get and your experience in property investment. Obviously, it is a commercial building so they need 20-30% deposit, but they are keen to give you the money to refurbish the building even if it is in a few years' time. You will notice when you drive to those areas a sign that says, "This building is financed by TUHF."

===*Igor I am aware that if you develop properties and you develop more than 3 properties, you are required by the NHBRC to register as a developer or something to that extent. When it comes to investing in property is there something similar in place===*

All my properties are under a trust and as I told you earlier, I plan to leave all those properties with my kids. It does not really matter if it can be in your own name, company's name or a trust; you must just have an idea of what you want to do from the beginning. If you want to own the company forever, then keep it in a trust, if you want to speculate then open a company or use your own name. It all depends on your strategy on how you want to invest in property.

===do you manage these properties yourself and who takes care of the maintenance===

After all the years, I have a good plumber, electrician, painter and all those other people. So if there is a burst pipe, I am not going to do it myself, I send a plumber. A trick is when those people send you an invoice, pay it immediately because if they know that when they do work for you they are paid immediately, they will be quick to attend to your problem. It terms of management I just go to the property every month to see if they are keeping the property in a good condition and those kinds of things. I also check if there are not too many people residing in the flat. Funny enough I have people staying in my flats for years; I have one or two staying in them from the time that I bought it in

2005. Sometimes I check my accounting books and see that they have paid hundreds of thousands in rent. The guy that rents the place I used to stay in before I moved to this house has paid R600 000 in rent already, it's ridiculous. You know people can be for or against property investment, but if somebody gives you R600 000 in 5years, that is something else.

===*any challenges in the property market currently, you have mentioned the age of the buildings and we hear on the news of water supply problems around Jo'burg*===

Personally, for me the biggest challenge is not being able to get a loan from the bank. Secondly in Jo'burg it can happen that they hi-jack the building, but that does not happen in the buildings that are nicely run; it happens in the buildings that are neglected by the owners. Somebody will see that the building is neglected and that is normally when there is no electricity; running water and then the tenants start asking what are they paying rent for then. Then some clever gang member, mafia comes, takes the building, and runs it for himself. There is mostly a problem with maintenance, but if there are proper trustees and managing agents, then all those problems get resolved. I am serving on three or two buildings as a trustee. If there is a building that I see is going down, then I jump in on the board and try to assist to fix it. In one of the buildings, I bought a flat in 2006 and in 2007; it was one of the best buildings in Sunnyside with roses and all. Then suddenly in about 3 years, the building went down so fast and so dramatically. Now I am on the board for about a year and a half, fixing so many things, but it is still a problem.

===*Is there a way that you time the property market and decide that you are now buying or now you just sit on your hands*===

There is an old saying that says if there is blood on the street, you buy property, but from my experience, I think the best time to buy a property is when the interest rates are high because people are too scared to buy. I was buying on auctions when the interest rates were about 15.5% just a few years back. On many properties, I was bidding alone. Funny story is that I was at an auction for some other reason and I was chatting to some people. I listened to the guy bidding for a bachelor flat in Boksburg CBD; I was never in the Boksburg area before then. It went from R60 000 to R70 000 and I thought to myself you cannot buy a bachelor flat in Hillbrow for that kind of money, why would Boksburg CBD be worse. I got the flat for R80 000 and the rent was R2600 at that stage already, now it is more than R3000. Currently I am not buying any property I am just collecting the cash and when the interest rate goes up and they will go up for sure; I will start buying, that could be in 2years or 4years time I will have a nice capital base. At that point everybody is afraid, the owners, banks, they will just give you the property for close to nothing.

===*currently what's your property portfolio like*===

At this stage, it is close to 50 or thereabout.

===*that must be quite difficult to manage. I think we have covered most of the hidden cost like special levies and so on, but is that all*===

Always put aside about 10% of the monthly rent aside. I do not use it that is only for covering shortfalls. For example, last month I had a lady-tenant that fell and broke her leg. She had to go to the hospital to amputate her leg and she could not pay her rent; she told me this on the 4th of August. I told her its fine; I mean what can I do? So you must have a little on the side for emergency in any case. It could be a special levy, a busted pipe or tenant leaving without telling you.

===*Igor what key annual events could one look out for and coming to my mind at the moment are things like interest rates going up, municipality increasing tariffs*===

Rates and taxes go up annually; you have levies that go up. Every four or five years they do a valuation of the property and this could affect your rates watch out for that. Luckily, those municipalities are getting a bit more technical now so you can download everything from the internet now. So every time they do the valuation I always go and complain and try to keep them down. In addition, your rent goes up every year so that covers you a bit. Interest rates you cannot foresee unfortunately, but if you have a nice cash positive property portfolio that is not going to affect you that much. If you get R2000 a month in your pocket or R1200, the difference is not that much. You have to look at it as a business and every business goes through cycles, as would your big shops like Pick 'n Pay or Woolworths. You must just watch the cash flow and you must watch that you do not run into a problem where you cannot pay the bond because if you do not pay for 2months, you will have a serious problem.

===*you've said something about your friends saying that you are crazy to go and buy in that area and most of us really get freaked out when we hear comments like that. What made you continue===*

Somehow, I am glad that I can think with my own head, I can listen to everybody but in the end, I make my own decision. After going to Sunnyside and seeing that I am still alive, I now go there a few times a month. Most of those buildings have security, but I also do not go there at 12 midnight in any case. I get told that I have a strange accent sometimes.

===*when you came to SA you had a job offer, how did that go and when did you stop working at that company===*

The company had very nice prospects, unfortunately wrong management was appointed and the company went down; especially in this industry, you must be very innovative. You must be able to move in front of everybody else and unfortunately, that did not happen. We started working for 4 days a week and then 3 days. Fortunately, at that, stage I had already started trading making quite nice money there, had started a property portfolio and my wife was working. We eventually decided that enough is enough and obviously, as one door closes another one opens. I resigned in that company and not even 15 days later, the people I was doing work for in that old company approached me. They wanted me to do work for them on a contract basis and we are still keeping that relationship.

===was that a difficult choice there when you had to leave the company===

When I left that job, I thought I would never do any engineering work again, that I would just focus on trading and investing. Then this company came and it just happened very quickly.

===How long have you been trading for now===

Sometime in October 2003.

===*and how did you stumble across this in the first place*===

That book I read opened my mind for the first time. At the old company, I was working for there was a person that I would overhear calling his brokers. At that time, the internet was not too effective and one day I knocked on his door and asked him what he was doing. He explained and gave me two old books, one was Fundamental Analysis and the other one was Fundamental Investing. I started reading and at the beginning for me, fundamental analysis made more sense than technical. I then came across Fin24 and at that stage, it was Money Max, which led me to SA Warrants and that was run by Simon Brown at that stage. So I basically went to a one day course which was here in Pretoria and the course was Introduction to Warrants. Everything started from then and it was even before I started investing in property. I did not have money; the only money I put into trading was R6000 – R7000. For about 2years it just went up and down, it was ridiculous; eventually about 2 years later it started making sense.

===*were you already trading fulltime by then*===

No, I was working still and I was trading warrants end of day, basically doing analysis in the morning and trades in the evening. That is the time when Absa and

Standard Bank started with online share trading and the costs of trading became much cheaper than before. So I basically concentrated on trading warrants and Top40 Index and just took it from there.

===*from my personal experience when I started trading the losses were painful to deal with. What kept you going*===

Losses are always painful, not at the beginning only. Today they are even more painful than at the beginning. At the beginning, you do not know what you are doing so it is somewhat ok, but now you do and you still lose money. What happens is that I always trade with a stop loss and I never let any of my trades go pass it. I also really like to learn, to read and I never do anything without investigating it first. I also read books like the Market Wizard by Jack D. Schwager and I saw that if they can do it, so could I. I told myself it is just a process; people come into trading and think they are going to make R 1million in a month or two. It takes a lot of time, lot of patience and lot of nerves to succeed.

===*Igor most people I come across think trading is gambling, what's your take there*===

Gambling is good for the casinos. Nobody forces people to go and gamble at Sun City or whatever casino they choose to visit. Many people come to trading because of the excitement thinking that it is gambling and unfortunately, that is the wrong way to look at it. I started trading because it was something I would like to learn and to do in 20years time. I never for once thought that I would make R500 000 by the end of the month. That is the difference and the reason why the success rate is so slow. People do not want to take the effort to learn what trading is all about.

===so were there any courses that you attended===

I only attended two courses with SA Warrants where they were talking about technical analysis. I also went to Dr David Paul's courses, he is still one of the best traders in South Africa; that is about it and it has been mostly books. These days it is much easier to learn, there are blogs, Twitter and so on. In that stage, it was mainly chat forums and it would take you 3months to get a book from Amazon. Now you can download it with Kindle and it is available immediately.

===The process of entering and exiting a trade I normally tell my friends that it is like finding a wife that you can trust when things are good and bad. I know there are many successful traders out there and I just could not trust their trading systems. I had to go out there and find something that worked for me. Was this also the case with you===

Yes, I posted this morning something on Trading

Wisdom by Jack Schwager and it said, "There are a million ways to make money in the markets, the irony is that they are all very difficult to find." You have to find something that suite you, some people want to trade intraday, and others want to trade the markets once a week so they look at weekly charts only. I sit in front of the screen all day and it all depends on your personality. To be successful in this, you must find something that suites you the best. You cannot take my trading system and make money; chances are very slim that it will work for you. I am sharing all my trading systems publicly from the 7/21 and people do not follow it, so I just stopped doing it.

===*what is your trading style, intraday or overnight trading*===

I am trading intraday/overnight. I have positions I open in the morning and close in the evening, others I keep them for a few days.

===*there are people that think once they attend a course or pay R36 000 for a course they will not make losses*===

I was present when all my three boys were born, but that does not make me a gynaecologist.

===*A builder needs a shovel and maybe throw in a digger loader now and then. What do traders need*===

This is it in front of me two screens, a keyboard and a mouse. Most of the platforms are cheap and very easy to use. I trade the ALSI on Swordfish, which is available locally and is free; they just get money by you trading.

===*looking at annual events that occur and could have an impact on the stock market, what would you say they are*===

If you are trading stocks then obviously, the earnings report. I know of people in the United States that wait for the earnings report from certain companies and they trade those days only. I trade the ALSI and there is no earning report, each day is a new day. For the other people it is news on the stocks. There are great people on Twitter and on some blogs, follow them. I really think that there is no good or bad investment, there are good and bad investors. People do not want to spend the time that is required to get the results. You go to school to become a doctor and spend 8 years; it can come to 10 or 20years. You come to the market thinking in 20minutes you are going to succeed that is completely wrong.

===*I think a lot of people approach the market with that mentality. Igor, how do you deal with the drawdowns that come with trading?* ===

Actually as the time progresses, you learn more and it is not that difficult anymore. At the beginning, it was a disaster you know, broken mouse, keyboards and shouting. As the time progresses and you get better, you start to realize that the losing trades are a part of this life; there is not a single trader out there, who does not lose money. You start realizing that if you keep your losses small and you do the right things in the right way you will succeed. I am reading a lot about trading psychology because I really believe that a lot of trading is psychology. This is an ever-changing market and especially these days the market is so easily accessible. The entry these days has become so small, you can open an account with $100, and most probably, you will lose it all. You have to adapt, look for the new opportunities, but it is the same with any company. Coca-Cola started with making coke, now they have 100s of different drinks. They did not sleep on one drink and expect big results. They developed and adapted to the market.

===*Traders I often read of, have lost all their money at one point, did this ever happen with you*===

No, that never happened to me. Like I told you, I started with R7000 and the closest I came to being bust was R2000. I was trading small, that R7000 I was trading in small 3 portions. From R7000 it dropped to

R2000 and then it went to R20000, then to R10000. Then 2 years later I started to make some money and for the first time reached R100 000. Let us face it, self-confidence and ego is one of the things that are killing most of the people in trading.

===*what books, TV-shows or seminars would you recommend*===

Look I do not watch TV shows, expect for Simon Brown from time to time, but please do not tell him that. There are some books, which are really classics like Reminiscence of a Stock Operator, Market Wizards, and New Market Wizards. When it comes to blogs, you must find what really suites you depending on your style of trading. Personally, I like to read about trading psychology and there is Dr. Brett Steenbarger on Traderfeed. That is what I start my day with and see what they published. Look around Twitter, you cannot follow 2000 people and get anything from it. If 2000 people tweet 5 times a day, that is 10000 tweets and there is no way you can follow all that.

===*you started trading with R7000, do you think it is possible to start with that amount these days*===

When I think about it now, I think it was crazy in that stage. The good thing these days is if you want to trade the ALSI, there is a product called the ALMI, which is $1/10^{th}$ of the ALSI. A good friend of mine wanted to find out how much must they put to start trading, I told him to put R5000 and trade the ALMI. That will allow him a 5000 points drawdown and he must be prepared to lose it all; there is a good chance he will. Do not put R50 000 and trade the ALSI, that will be R50 000 gone in 2months, that is going to destroy you and you will never go back into the market. You also get to create demo accounts, but trading demo account is not the same as trading live. Your first job in the stock market is not to make money, it has to survive and not get broke. There are lot of products to trade from CFDs, stocks, options, futures, forex and millions of questions you have to answer before you start trading. If you put all your money at once, there is a good chance that you will lose it all. Take the total, and split it into small chunks and put little by little. That will give you much longer time to survive and maybe learn how to trade.

===So what do you enjoy the most about trading===

It is finding out new things, it feels you with satisfaction when you find out things that work better than the things that worked before; finding news, new markets to trade and learning. Trading is a magnifying glass of your life, you inner being and emotions. If you did not sleep well, had a fight with your wife, kids, were stuck in traffic, you will trade better that day for sure. Improving in trading for me is equal to improving myself as a father, husband or even a better neighbour.

===*so what are your days like these days*===

I wake up around 06:00 and take care of the baby while my wife takes the older ones to school. I am in front of the screen around 08:00 and watch the news to see what happened in the US overnight. From 08:30 until 17:30 it is trading, that is when I am mostly in front of the screen. Usually my phone is on silent or vibration during that time, I do not allow it to disturb me. At 17:30, I finish and if I have an overnight position, I come back around 20:30. Obviously, during that time I am updating on Trading Wisdoms. I also watch what is happening in the US not that I make decisions on what is happening there. It is mainly to see what how the markets there are doing.

===*you have mentioned Trading Wisdom a number of times, what is that about*===

Trading Wisdoms is my website that I started www.tradingwisdoms.com. For many years when I was reading books, I started writing down something I liked, be it a paragraph or a sentence. Twice a year I would go through them, and all of a sudden last year a thought crossed my mind how I could share this with other people. I already had a collection of about 1000 "wisdoms". The idea is to share what good traders have to say.

===*what was the response you got from the public*===

There are people that really enjoy them and retweet every single tweet. Funny enough, I got more response from the US trading community than here. I think it is because the US is more developed and there are many people trading there compared to South Africa. There are people that retweet them in big blogs there. For now, it is just a hobby; maybe I will make it more commercial in the future.

===*what is the one thing you learnt through your career*===

I would say hard work always pays. You must work hard and you must know what you are doing and not take stupid risks. Even with the kids as well, spend enough time with them.

===*I am guessing you get a lot of free time these days*===

Yes a lot, because it is much easier. At the start I watched every single tick and stayed up at night to watch the US market. I just control the risk now and even if something happens that I did not expect, I will not lose my house.

===*A quick question on the properties is there a number that you will stop at. I mean 50 is quite a lot*===

No, not even 10% of my time is spent on property. It is for my kids, to leave them with something so they can pay lobola (bride price) one day. Who knows, they can pay with property and not cows.

===*what advice would you give to new investors*===

If you want to spend time learning how this works, do it and do it with your full heart. If you are not willing to spend time, buy Satrix40, you will not lose money. Do not think you will become a millionaire by tomorrow, put hard work, put your heart to it, learn, learn and learn.

===*Igor what happened to the electrical engineer*===

From time to time when I have spare time, I do it at night; this is my passion, property investing and trading. Sometimes when I am not doing so well in the market I ask myself why did I not pursue a career in the corporate world; but I guess I would not be able to sit in shorts next to my kids all day long.

-----------------------------------END-------------------------

I contacted Igor in the very first stages of conducting the interviews and at the time, I was still filled with a lot of doubt and lacking an indication if what I was doing would help anyone. He was by far quite welcoming and interested in taking the interview and he believed that the country needed more effect to drive it further in terms of entrepreneurship. As mentioned earlier I had never met Igor so I was nervous as I drove to his house in Pretoria. I arrived at his residence an hour early and he was one of the few people I found to have been working from his residence. I parked in front of his garage in an upmarket estate and I could feel the envy starting to build inside me. He was one of the few people that remembered my name when I met him. My first comment to him was about the fact that it is 14:00 and he was in shorts and sneakers. He responded by saying he was at gym, he has a home gym and the envy grew more inside me. We stopped in his office, which was by far the neatest office I had ever seen in my life, and everything was neatly packed in an orderly manner. This reminded me of the trading charts, he often puts up on social networks, and they were neat and not clustered. As with all the interviews, I wanted to find out as much I could from this gentleman, but time was a limiting factor. At the end of the interview, he speaks about how he would not be able to spend time with his kids if he had a full time job. During the interview his kids came back from school and came rushing in his office to greet him and I could see they wanted to spend some time with him. While this was happening I quickly recalled how he mentioned earlier that he would sometimes spend time at his dad's office and that was where his love for economics slowly developed. A couple of months later after the interview I chatted with him via email once again about why he stopped trading the ALSI instrument and his response was that he wanted to spend more time with his kids. I am mentioning this because I think we all need a pivot point to centre ourselves around, something that takes us away from the insanity of chasing money, something to look up to when times are tough. For Igor, it is his family; for me, it is being free from ties that bind. For someone else it might be religion and others it might be spending time with the needy. We are told a number of times how property is a great investment and this gets embedded in us so much that one forgets to do all the necessary research. We blindly follow this without taking the time to think why are we doing it and what kind of investment best suits our investing style. Before meeting Igor, I would have never in my wildest dreams bought property where he bought because of what I have been told, "Buy in new developments and not in the urban zone of decay." He mentions two things around this his decision-making and the first is that he never does anything without investigating it first. The second one is that he always makes his own decisions and not influenced by other people. I must also admit that if I were his friend when he went to buy the first property, I would have also advised him against it. It is important that we do not let other people influence our decision-making.

I have never read Rich Dad, Poor Dad, but I have heard a lot of people talk about it. What I can say is that from that small sample I have heard very few people actually going out and practising what they read from it. Trading in the stock market is by far one of the most self-challenging professions there is and requires an awful lot of discipline. I have struggled on this journey and after this interview my approach to trading changed. He points out a few things in the interview and the first one is that he approached trading as something he wanted to do in 20years time. I learnt that we rush things, wanting to see the results tomorrow and life does not always work like that. Applying this on my trading, it allowed me room to understand that things take time and I can do this if I do not rush it. The second one is that he never does anything without investigating it first, this allowed me to spend a bit more time on my research and finding out why things work the way they do. The third is about finding things that work better than before. The only way to come up with original ideas is to come with solutions to existing problems, improvement on current systems.

Sometimes we watch a movie and right at the beginning they show a person wearing a red cap and if you do not pay attention or miss the red cap, you have missed the whole point of the movie. Right at the end, they show this person once again and all of a sudden, the light bulb goes on. This applies in some areas of our lives as well. Igor read books and kept on collecting quotes or wisdoms as he calls it, he did not know why at the start, but sharing them with other people was that light bulb moment. We may not understand why we do certain things or have the drive to do them, in the end it all connects if we keep an open mind.

LANGA MBULAWA OF MBULAWA & SONS

INTRODUCTION: I am in a small town called Cala, in the Eastern Cape chatting to Langa Mbulawa of Mbulawa & Sons. We grew up calling him TaMla and still call him so; The "Ta" is from the so-called Tsotsi Taal, which depicts Grootman or Older Brother. For the purpose of this interview, I will refer to him as TaMla. I grew up knowing him as local a schoolteacher, but his life really changed in the past couple of years.

===*TaMla I remember growing up and seeing you around town as a schoolteacher, your life has changed quite significantly since. First things first, can you share who is TaMla, where you grew up and went to school*===

Let me start by greeting you Mkhwane(Litha's clan name) and everyone out there. I am Langa Mbulawa, I was born in a village called Lower Cala a few kilometres out of town. I did my primary school in Cala River and I went to a local school called Cala Village. From there I did my high school in Cala High School famously known as eMamfene then. After completing my high school I went to Lumko College of Education where I was trained to be a teacher. I then returned to Cala Village as a teacher. I worked as a teacher up until early this year (2014) where I decided to retire from teaching.

===*Wow! Retiring at such an early age. I know over a dozen people who would love to retire early, but cannot. Was this always something that you wanted to do*===

It was not easy Litha, it was not easy at all. Due to certain circumstances regarding that had to do with the line of business I chose, they led to me making a difficult choice. I had to choose between being a civil servant or be self-employed. There were certain challenges whereby if you are a government employee, you cannot do business with the state. Like I said, it was not an easy decision, but eventually I had to choose a side.

===*it sounds like a tough choice one has to make around such, I can just hear from the way you keep on reiterating this. During your school years, would you say there were other career paths you were interested in following*===

Litha, I would be lying if I were to say there were any, those years when I went to school the only careers that we were made aware of are teaching, nursing or a police. I was part of that generation and yes, other opportunities were made available to us later on when I was already employed as a teacher. So out of the three careers I chose the one of being a teacher.

===*if I heard clearly, you mentioned that you went to school at Cala Village and then later went back to teach there, how was that experience like when you came back*===

I really appreciated it because I was once a scholar there and going back to an environment that I am familiar with, made me much happier. You know most schools have cultures and you arrive there as a student and you find this culture, coming back as teacher you come back to a culture you know. Moreover, some of the teachers that were there are teachers that taught me as a student, so I really adjusted there very well.

===*looking at the business side, you often find people at work be it now teachers or a secretary selling maybe sweets or biscuits. Would you say that you have done something like that*===

I could say I grew up around businesses because we had a spaza shop at home. Even when I was in college I sold cigarettes at the residence I was staying at so I could have a bit of pocket money. I was also partly involved in the taxi business because we had taxis at home, I do not think I have never been separated from it. What I picked up from other people at the time was that if their parents sold vetkoeks, they would try to distance themselves from that business. They would forget that these are the same vetkoeks that made it possible for them to go to school. So I really tried working with my old man and still work together with him even at this very stage.

===*referring to what you just said about working together with your dad, did that help you a lot to in terms of guidance and mentorship? I think it forms a crucial part when starting out to have someone who you can consult in times of difficulties*===

Having a father like the one I have has really been helpful to me because to this very day he still helps me out a lot in some of the things. In as much as I have been involved in this business, there are things that I still do not know. I also told myself that in times of difficulty, we will hold each other's hand and find a way forward together.

TaMla sometimes we tend to think that if we set up shop today while living in a rondavel, next week we will be staying in a mansion. Particularly referring to myself also here that sometimes I think this will make me a quick buck. From your experience, would you say that you thought this will expand quickly or you just took it as it came?

You see Litha when we start getting there, that is one of our problems as people. For example, another person might see this Langa or TaMla people talk about and think that it has been an easy path. Even people who know me well know that it has not been an easy path, it's a long road and remains long. I remember as a child that only car that my dad had back then was "Inculancula" (a 1976 Toyota minibus taxi). Some people might not even know what that is or what type of minibus that is. What I am trying to say is that it has been a long road. Some will start a business today and think that they will quickly be like Langa, who seems like he is maybe in the right direction. Even now, there are difficulties. At times, it feels like you are climbing a steep hill and at times you are on flat terrain, but not downhill yet.

===*there is something I like joking about with my friends. I have noticed that your peers do buy and change cars a lot, but the only personal car I recall you driving is an old maroon Nissan Sabre, what happened to it if I may ask*===

I remember that car, that was the first car I bought for myself, but due to the ever-changing times, I traded it in. I was still young back then; it was only a 1600 engine, so I bought myself a Nissan Sentra that had more power with a 2.0litre engine.

===*from there I do not recall you having another car until recently when you bought yourself a van. Was this a way of preserving capital or were you not interested in the modern cars*===

Litha our taste as human beings is very different. After the second Sentra, I felt like I have now lived my youth. I decided that I should get a car that is going to help me carry out some of the work I had. Personally, I think a van is better than a sedan as it can help bring in income.

===*it makes a lot of sense. Tell us about the company name. I have seen some taxis around town with two different names Mbulawa & Son and Mbulawa Tours. Which one is your company and what is it that you do*===

There is only one company, Mbulawa & Son; Mbulawa Tours is our marketing strategy. They all belong to one company.

===*and then what other line of business are you currently involved in? I have also seen your van towing a trailer a couple of times*===

I have tried to expand the business into other areas as well trying to avoid having all my eggs in one basket. I am involved in the transport, toilet hire services and trying to expand that also. I started supplying fruit to the government schools after I saw that the government wanted to introduce fruit as part of the feeding scheme at schools. When the local Spar Supermarket burnt down, I saw an opportunity. I found out that most of the schools bought fruit from Spar, so I saw a gap and took it.

===*that is a gap I did not even see TaMla. I think it is easier for us humans to go copy something that is already in existence than to take on such windows of opportunity. Quite often, us as the youth struggle due to that. You were the first person in town to start the toilet hire service, how did you get that right*===

Well I travel a lot to Cape Town and on one of my visits there, I saw a company called Mshengu Toilet Hire. I worked out that this could be a way to make extra money. I also noticed that there were no Mshengu's here in Cala, let me perhaps try this out. My friends were also laughing at me because I was doing business with toilets. I would tell them that if we were to all stand at the till to pay for something, my money smells the same as theirs, how I made it is irrelevant. The shop will not reject mine because it comes from "Mshengu." That part of the business gets busy and I have to turn customers away. That was just a gap I saw and I capitalised on it.

===*i think we struggle to see other things because we think it is a stupid idea and it will not work. My great grandfather would have probably laughed at something like that. Times are changing and we need to keep up. Getting to the name, you have split them to Mbulawa & Son, which is just a general dealer and can do all kinds of work; you then changed the other one to Mbulawa Tours. Was there perhaps a different market you were targeting with this approach===*

Mbulawa & Son is the name that we used in the taxi business. You will find that with most big companies they tend to change their branding. For example, PEP will maybe change their logo a bit just to keep up with times and trying to attract the younger people. You sometimes have to bring out what people want to see.

===when you invest your own capital into something new, you sometimes get sleepless nights thinking about the risk you have taken. Did you by any chance experience this in the earlier stages===

As I mentioned earlier it was a tough decision that I had to make, fortunately there are people who inspired me. Yes, the fear of the unknown comes naturally. Once you take the decision, you have to understand that there is no other place that you will receive your bread from. Your bread gets buttered where you are now and there is no turning back. You have to wake up and work hard.

===just a quick question, I have heard that one needs to pay a

joining fee to enter the taxi industry which can be excessive. Is this only applicable in certain towns or route===

That is one of the difficult issues to discuss because that joining fee is not standard. Sometimes this is done for just blocking people into the industry. This fee does not even guarantee you a return in the future. If for example, you buy a taxi today and tomorrow the insurance company writes it off, you joining fee does not get refunded.

===in terms of funding, where you would suggest that one should go to? I have heard of companies like South African Taxi Finance and then you have your normal banks===

People must use their own discretion, but I would advise people to go for the long-standing banks. Some people just go for any institution without looking at things like the interest rate. I would advise people to shop around and see what options they can get. It is easy to acquire a car; it is difficult to keep up with the payments. These days they even make it easy and just call you unexpectedly and offer you a car, people often fall for this. Everyone gets excited when purchasing a new car and when told to sign quickly, they will do so without even looking at what they are signing for.

===do you do mainly long distance or local trips? Maybe just go further and share why you made that choice===

As I have said that, it has been a while since I have been involved in this business and the people of Cala really try to support me. Most of my work is organised tours and special trips. I mainly deal with them; I occasionally do long distance trips. Long distance trips are a seasonal business that I do during the busy times of the year like the Easter Weekend, June Holidays and December when people take extended leave from work.

===*organised trips, is this now schools and government trips only*===

It is schools, government departments, weddings, funerals, etc.

===*I am still very new when it comes to employing people. What would you say is the best way to deal with employees*===

I cannot say it is because I pay better, but I still have the same employees I started with. I have not been in a situation where one of them left or I have fired them. Yes, I do get problems here and there, but they are still young men and do have challenges. Sometimes you find that they did not make it in time for a trip because they had a late night like most young men. Maybe you could even ask them because if they were not happy, they would have left me already.

===*looking at most businesses there are certain events that occur annually that could affect operations. Such will be things like government spending, interest rate hike and the like. What would say those things are in your line of business? How does one navigate through such things*===

The support I get from people and government really helps me to get through such. With government, I know that I will have to wait a while before I get paid due to their internal processes, but I see that as money already in the bag.

The toughest times of the year are May, August and October in this industry. People are not travelling as they used and one of the attributing factors is that they are unemployed. If people are unemployed, we have no one to transport. Even the long trips that we do, is mostly transporting people who were on holiday and are going back to their jobs. Now if there are no jobs, this affects us a lot.

===*what I would like to look at is things like fuel price increase, things that someone from outside would not be aware of*===

In South Africa, you find that petrol price can go up 3 times within 4months. Now it is not easy for us to increase the fares every time the petrol price goes up. At times, we have to absorb three or four fuel price increases before we increase our fares. It is a painful situation because when the price of fuel goes up, the oil price goes up, I think even the price of tyres goes up. We do try to be lenient at times and absorb increases for a whole year and only increase our fares in December.

===*well you supply fruit to a number of places and I think you carry the risk of making sure that they arrive fresh. Is that side of the business always busy*===

Litha it depends on the harvesting times. What happens with apples for example is that when they harvest the prices are low because the supply exceeds the demand. Then later in the year, you find that the prices start to increase because the supply is low. In addition, you must remember that they also keep them in cold storage at a cost to them as well.

===*TaMla I have been watching your working style for the past couple of days I have been around town. It seems quite relaxed in a spectator's view, I might be wrong. I have also noticed that you no longer drive the taxis yourself. Kindly take us through a typical workday, understanding that we all need to wake up to earn our keep*===

Mkhwane(Litha's clan name), as you also said we all have to wake up, otherwise I would be sleeping on the job. I have to wake up like everyone else going to work because I have to make sure that everything runs smoothly. For example if there is a group of people that have organised transport with me, I have to make sure that my drivers arrive on time. I cannot relax just because I know that I told the drivers what they needed to do. I have to be there just in case I have to chip in and drive it myself. I am always on standby.

===*taking out one thing you have learnt from when you started till now, something you think might be valuable for someone else, what would it be*===

I have been on a long journey as I have mentioned from the time of Inculancula. In whatever one does, they must make sure that they are consistent. Understand that it is a long journey and you must not be extravagant, as I mentioned earlier that banks would even offer you a car while you were not looking for one. At the end of the month, the banks will always want their money. Do not think for a second that you have now arrived because you have two or three cars.

----------------------------**END**----------------------------

This was the very first interview I did, and as they, say anything that can go wrong will go wrong. I have known Langa since I was a child he was one of the teachers at the local schools. Approaching him seemed the easy thing to do and as it turned out, he was more than willing to contribute. The interview was set for 16:00 that afternoon and I was quite nervous myself as it was going to be my first interview. I remember rushing up and down a few minutes before the interview as the anxiety grew and losing my voice recorder and so on.

The interview begins and half way through it, I found that I was missing some pages and had to do with what I could remember. Since then I have learnt a lot on how to prepare and conduct myself, but I have also managed to learn from him as well. At the start of the interview, he does something different from all the other interviews by sending a greeting to all the people who will be reading this interview. As he recalls his days as a learner right through to when he became a teacher, he was covered with a smile on his face. This soon fades as he shares about the choice he had to make to leave his fulltime job and a sign of how difficult it was for him to leave his job. He had become part of the school's culture that he referred to at the beginning. One of the things I do admire about his story is the fact that he started his company while he was in a secure position and built it to what it is today. Often we tend to procrastinate, that we if we start a company we would have to leave our jobs, as we see here it is not always the case. Eventually the company will need more attention from one and the tough choice will have to be made. I mentioned the point about his old car because most people his age at the time were all buying fancy cars, he would buy secondhand cars and today this tells me he had a plan. One of the things I left out in the interview was that he has had other businesses that failed before or did not do so well, one I remember quite well was his bottle store. In the end, what has worked for him is going back to the industry he grew up exposed to, which was the mini bus business. He highlights a very important note when speaks of how people would not want to be associated with the businesses their parents were running. That really hit home in my case and as my dad had a dairy when I was growing up, I would get teased about this in school to a point I would not want to be associated with milk. Most people grew up with parents doing some kind of business and one does not really have to replicate what has been done, perhaps look for ways of improving on it. Finding ways to do things better, simpler using the same model used by our parents and off course those around us.

What has been interesting as well is the fact that he still managed to stay close to the teaching profession by doing school trips and working with the government. This tells me there could be a lot of opportunities within our current workspace we can look at, but that will also depend on what kind of a boss you have. On the other hand he shows another skill of being able to spot gaps in the market within the town itself without moving to bigger cities. He also shows the ability of keeping an open mind as he travels, one being the toilet hire service, the other supplying fruit. These are all things he saw while on his trips to Cape Town. Even though he operates within a small space, he is willing to grow and venture into other businesses. He also points out something many are faced with when starting something new, friends that will doubt what you are doing or even laugh at it as with the case with him. No one can ever share our vision for what we are trying to achieve, it is our goal to show them by just doing. One of the main lessons I learnt from the interview being consistence, the dangers of credit, mentorship, keeping an open mind.

LYNETTE BARNES OF CAPE HONEY FACTORY

INTRODUCTION: I first met Lynette about a year ago. She had managed to do some restoration work on this old neglected property and really brought it back to life. She really did a stunning job and she did this without demolishing most of the structure. I soon learnt that she is a beekeeper and produces honey. It was the first time that I came across some who was doing this at a commercial scale. It kind of reminded some years back as a boy of how we used to go from one beehive to the next trying to get honey. And make no mistake I made sure that I stood at a safe distance while waiting for my friends to bring me some honey.

But then again as with everything in life, we prefer to be safe and expect people to bring us what we want and at times, we tend to wait forever.

===*Lynette the last time I was on the farm you mentioned that you like nature and more especially trees. You even went as far as building your veranda around an existing tree to avoid cutting it. Any idea when your passion or love for nature started*===

I think I grew up with that, my father was a great nature lover. We did not stay on a farm or anything, but my father would take us to places like Knysna Bush where you have a lot of trees. So I learnt from him about the trees, I am not claiming to know all the trees, but I do know that they are not there to be cut off.

===*And you managed to find a way of making a living from nature without causing too much damage to the natural state; well I hope that is the case*===

My husband's father was a beekeeper and I met him while we were in the police. Eventually, he started doing bee keeping as well and that was the perfect thing for me because at the time I was considering what I would do after my career as a police. I saw this as a great opportunity to start bee keeping and doing the management of the business. So we started doing it fulltime and everything that goes with bee keeping.

===*what do you mean by everything that has to do with bee keeping? And perhaps, just take me through the process and what you guys do. A number of things popping up in my mind like breeding, producing the honey and sending it off to the shelves===*

Our business for us is not something we do to make money, bees are something we love, and they are a part of nature. How you start is catching the bees by putting hives outside and we attract the bees using wax and propolis. So we attract them and at certain times of the year they swarm off to the wild bees and if they find the hive that is attractive they will move in if the queen is with them; the queen is mostly with them. That is how you get the bees, it's not something you can just fetch or buy at the shops.

===assuming this is more like farming, is there a specific time of the year that one needs to do this or you can just do it throughout the year===

It is more in spring, which is the time of the year that bees normally swarm off. You will see them also in trees around that time of the year and you get people who will not want them in their trees; it is very difficult to get them out. So what we do, is we try to attract them off the unwanted places, climb up the trees sometimes shake them off.

===now there is something I do not think I would try. Lynette on my previous chats with you, you mentioned that there is a huge demand locally for honey and that there is not enough honey to export. Do you think that there is a gap in the market for

newcomers===

Definitely, there are constantly people from overseas that want our honey because it is so natural and pure, but there are regulations in which some of the European countries do not accept South African honey. There is definitely a market and I know of people who export honey especially this fynbos honey.

===now you have lost me, I thought there was one type of honey and now you are talking about fynbos honey. Are there different types of honey===

You do get different types of honey; each flower gives a different taste. The bees make honey from the nectar and the most popular in the Western Cape is the blue-gum eucalyptus; that is one of the trees we are trying to protect, because everybody wants to cut them down. In the Citrusdal area, you get the citrus honey, which is not orange, but the colour is very light and sweet kind of honey. You get honey that is called borgo, which does not have a very nice taste, but fynbos is more to the Hermanus side and the bees make honey from it. In the Western Cape, alone you get over 22 types of honey.

===would I be thinking along the right lines if I say your target market are retailers in the likes of Pick & Pay, Shoprite and so on===

That's right companies like Pick 'n Pays, Spar and

Shoprite. You also get companies that use honey for cereals, they also form part of our client base.

===*every company has to take inventory to survive and I do not think yours is something you can easily measure like a herd of cattle*===

That is one of the problems because you cannot really say that you have a swarm of bees; they can easily decide tonight that they do not like this place and they move on. They will just decide that they are going to another place and you cannot do anything to keep them. So they are only there because they want to be there not because we trap them.

===*that must require some kind of love and caring then*===

Yes, when there is caring and food they will stay; if that does not happen they will live the place.

===*then it comes to shelf space with the retailers, I immediately think of wine. I know wine makers often have to prove themselves to get shelf space. Would you say that it is the same when it comes to wine*===

It is not so easy we struggled long ago with Pick 'n Pay and we are now struggling with Checkers. One of the threats is imported honey that is being sold cheaper to the traders. This keeps South African honey off the shelves because of the prices and as you said earlier, you thought there is one type of honey.

===*I must say that for a lady I would expect something like a nursery, obviously I am wrong. I know my niece would run outside at the sight of a bee inside the house. How was it for you the first time you came across a swarm of bees*===

It was scary and still scary even now because at times they get more aggressive. Sometimes you are in a vehicle, two or three bees come inside and you do not know the first place to cover. At times when you least expect them to be aggressive and are not wearing any protective clothing, the next moment they are all over you.

===*That reminds years back as a teenager driving with my mother through a bushy area with the windows open and out of the blue, we had a swarm of bees inside the car. We had to jump out of the car very fast, that was quite an experience. What year did you start with this and how long was it before you could say that you are breaking even*===

We had been doing bee keeping for some time, but we officially went commercial in 2008 and started bottling honey around the same time. It takes a while to get together especially if you do not have enough capital. It can be very pricey and as I said earlier, you never know if the bees will stay with you or not. Normally people start with 2 hives and build on from there. I would say not in the first 2years, you would still get your honey, but not to say that you will be making a living from it. It is a gradual thing because there is a time where you will not want to do bee keeping, but it grows in you.

===*I think the gradual is of importance because most of the time we want to skip the slow process and get straight to making* ===*money*

There are people like that. You know last year we had to make hives for people and although they are not beekeepers, they wanted to have five hives within a year. For me, you cannot do that especially if you are not a trained beekeeper. Even if you get the necessary training, you need to have the passion, love and knowledge. You can only learn by doing it yourself.

===*so is there a special type of training needed*===

There is no specific training, but we are going to start basic training so people at least know what to look for.

===*you have the bees and you have the hive, is there a specific machinery needed for this type of work*===

When you are starting out you do not need machines, you can cut out the honey and put it in the sun. There is ways you can extract the honey, but when you grow, you need the machines. You will also need a smoker when collecting the honey and all that does is to make them calm as they will not sting you. It is necessary have.

===*Most of the times when we are planning to start something new, we are most likely going to start by listing all the things that could go wrong and never really get to put anything into action. I could just sum it up to fear. Were you ever worried that something might go wrong===*

I never think of things that can go wrong, I just want to see the positive side. Yes, I know people get stung and can get allergic overnight from bee stings. Maybe there was a fear of the unknown, but I have always told myself that we will make it.

===from a distance, most jobs look easy until you actually get to do it yourself. I thought this would be one of the easy ones until I read that people get stung and sweat a lot under the protective gear. You have mentioned being stung yourself, what makes you keep going===

I am not scared of the bees; yes, I know there are people who are. I get stung often; I was just stung by a bee about a week ago. You do not want to get stung, but it is part of your job. You keep going back because it feels good to be doing it, and because you are passionate about it.

===More often than not when you are starting out a new venture you have that one person or two who are always pessimistic about your plans. They will go to great lengths pointing out all the negative things. Would you say you had one of those and how did you get over such===

Definitely had a lot of those especially in the job that I had. I was in the police at the time and now going to do something very different. There were people that asked me how I could go from being a station commissioner to being a beekeeper. I just thought that I am not going to let myself down on this, it is something I wanted to do and I decided that I would do it. Yes, I still miss the police and the action there, especially tonight when the president will be opening the parliament officially for the year. So yes, you get people especially friends that say you will not make it or are you not afraid and how will you survive. Others were saying that bee keeping is such a tough job, but I think that is where my experience in the police came in. Like working at night when we do pollination, we take the bees to the required farm in the dark; it can be hard work. You can only do it at night or very early in the morning before the sun comes out. You will be busy working the whole day and when it is dark, you will start and you finish off at 04:00 in the morning. That in its own requires determination.

===*so does that mean they are sleeping at night*===

They are sleeping and calm at night. During the day, they will come out and sting the people in the vehicle

===*at some point I guess you have to hire people, how long does it take to train someone to a point where one can confidently leave them unattended*===

It takes more than a year just to do the basic. You see, you constantly learn while you are going through this.

===*earlier you mentioned that people rush things and want to have 500 hives within a year, how many hives do you currently have, given the fact you have been operating for plus 7years*===

We had about 2000, but every year after pollination, we lose some. Also now, with the current epidemic American Foulbrood (AFB), we will have to count again after this season to get them ready.

===*so you lose them completely after the pollination*===

They will be tired, which is one of the reasons they die and some will fly away.

===*and you cover that in your costs*===

Yes. Then there are things like vandalism where people break in to steal the honey; not only people, but animals too like the badges. The veldfires also play a role, because you are not always there.

===*staff numbers required to look after 2000 hives*===

We have about 13 people.

===*Lynette what are the main challenges one can come across. Things that come to my mind are special permits, maybe a special board or body one needs to register with to make it commercially*===

The biggest challenge currently is the AFB and that is killing the bees. If you do not have bees, you will have no honey. The other challenge is the honey that is imported. If you have a lot of honey in your hands, it is sometimes not easy to sell it due to the cheaper honey imported. For exporting, some countries do not accept South African honey.

===*is there a fixed market price for honey. We know with things like gold, we have a fixed international price*===

It varies between commercial beekeepers and the retailers. The price is currently about R40 a kilogram, but imported honey is about R20 a kilogram.

===*so problems like the current epidemic would then obviously push the prices higher in terms of supply and demand*===

Yes, they do get higher, but I must stress that the honey is not infected. It is just the bees that get infected, the sickness is not carried through. It does affect the numbers though.

===*I believe you are also the chairwoman of the Western Cape Beekeepers Association, (that is a long name) what does your job there entail*===

I am the coordinator of the beekeepers in the Western Cape. It's an association where beekeepers register and know what to do when things are not going well in the industry. Our organisation is there so that people can learn from each other.

===*you have worked for the South African Police Service*

(SAPS), how long were you there for===

I was there for 30years. I started as a constable and I moved up with the ranks. I got my diploma in the police, I was the first female lieutenant in the Western Cape, and as I moved ranks, I moved from one police station to another. I ended up in Cape Town Central as a station commander.

===you continue to prove me wrong as a female, it must have been tougher when you started out, what made you choose the career at the time===

Strange, I never thought I would do the police work at the time, but my brother was a police officer. He had just come out of the training college and one evening he was chatting to his friend about the new recruits who happened to be women. It was very strange for them that there were now women in the police force. As I was listening to them, I decide that I also want to join the police and the next day I went to the local police station to apply. At that time it was very strict and each woman that applied, they had to go through a board, which would interview them. It was quite difficult back then to join the police as a female and the courses were very strict. We had 6months of training, which is very tiresome because you are always running.

===like a concentration camp===

Not that bad, but it was hard.

===*You eventually worked your way up the ranks, how did you find it when you had to give orders to your sub-ordinates; that is now assuming that a lot of them were males. Was it easy and did you quickly earn their respect*===

It was difficult at first, but they soon learnt that you don't just get handed the rank, you work for it and you have the required experience. It does happen that nowadays people get higher ranks without the relevant experience; you do not earn respect like that. What made it easy is that the police force is a disciplined organisation and you have to respect the rank more than you do the person. Then off course if you are not doing your job, they will not respect you, it is mainly the way that you represent yourself.

===*you mentioned one of my favorite words there "discipline." Has that kind of discipline helped when you went to start on your own*===

To start your own business is tough; you need to have a vision and the plan to get there. It is easy to say I have no one instructing me, so I will not work today. You have to discipline yourself that you will work today, you will do the pollination tonight and when you come back from that, you will do the rest of the work. I think that in any business you need that. Sometimes you will watch people going out for a meal or having fun; you have nothing keeping you here, but you know you have to do it.

===*The experience with your sub-ordinates in terms of decision making of which I am sure sometimes you needed to be strict, has that helped with your current staff members. More especially in the lines handling quarrels, non-performance and people not showing up for work*===

I think my biggest learning curve was in the police, especially with discipline. I sometimes tend to think that my staff must also respect my rank, but they are not in the police. They do know that there are disciplinary measures with certain incidents, but I also make certain that I do not overdo it.

===*that is one of the things we struggle with. I worked with someone that had a problem of coming to work late; eventually I had to stand up. It is never a nice feeling because right after that you have to work with that person again*===

Yes, I know exactly the feeling.

===*of the tough decisions you have had to make while you were a station commissioner, would you remember any tough calls you had to make*===

There were a number of incidents where I had to decide what my next move would be. An example would be taxi violence, how do you handle a situation without shooting? The biggest one was a hostage situation in Cape Town. The person took his girlfriend hostage at the restaurant where she was working. He came in, shot a few people and luckily did not kill anyone. We were there for almost 12 hours, so we were talking to this person the whole time trying to get him to set the woman free. Eventually, when he did things to her that made us aware the he could shoot her, I had to make the decision whether we were going to go in and shoot him before he shoots her or not. That was a tough decision to make.

===*That sounds tough. I read somewhere that you decided to take early retirement from your job, was this an easy decision to make and did you have it planned out from the start*===

No, it was not easy I loved my job. My last day at work I arrived at 06:00, and people were asking if was I really leaving, and why was I so early? I just thought it was the right time, it was not a matter of ok, now I am tired of that; I loved the police work until the end. I thought of my future and this was something that had to do with nature, which I loved, and it came at the right time.

===*you mentioned a few times already how you miss the police work, what would be the one thing you miss the most*===

I miss the action, working outside, the smokkelhuis (taverns) all the way from Kuils River to Mfuleni and Eerste River. I miss going to close illegal shebeens (taverns) during weekends, looking for illegal firearms and the marches to the parliament. I miss the people I worked with and their company.

===*I can imagine I went from an office with plus 60 people to sitting all by myself. I often make an example of how I ended up being an aimless drifter with no direction. I make an example of how I came to Cape Town to study and ended up settling without even planning that. Going back to what you said that you worked your way up the ranks, did you always have a fixed plan of how you wanted things to be one day*===

Yes, I always wanted to grow in my ranks and be the best I could be within the police. I always worked towards the direction of the next promotion, although I did not know where I would be stationed with the promotion, I had the desire to achieve. As I said, I thought the time was right to go and start something that I could for the rest of my life.

===*has the way in which you handled problems in your policing job changed now that you're working for yourself; would you say your skills have changed much*===

It changed. There are rules in the police that do not necessarily work well in the private sector. I had to make some little adjustment and I cannot use my ranks when it comes to ordinary people especially with the bees. Yes, the basic principles are there same. In the police people would salute when I pass, now here, things are not the same.

===*We hear war stories of people failing when they try out new ventures more than those of people who make a success; do you think it's because we turn a blind eye on the success? And perhaps not wanting to learn from the successful people===*

People tend to think more about the negative side of things and it really takes a special person to go over those types of things and not fail. It is easier to fail than to succeed, but you need a little bit more determination than people do even if everything goes against you.

===looking at your past experiences, what lessons are there that you could share with other people===

To succeed you must carry on doing what you are doing and never give up even if everything is against you; also, there will always be people who will say you are going to fail. Another thing is the money you get in you cannot go and spend it in one go; put it back into your business. That is one of the reasons people fail, they cannot work with money or think they can go spend it now and tomorrow will take care of itself; I do not believe in that.

===earlier, you mentioned how your dad loved nature. Would you say that he was your mentor or maybe there are other people who have been your inspiration===

My father loved nature. My mother was a very determined person and was the only woman in an attorney firm. She would put me on the back of her bicycle and take me to someone that would look after me and she would then cycle to her job. I remember one time I broke my leg because I fell on the spokes of the bicycle, even with the plaster she kept on carrying me on the bicycle. So I think my mother and brothers were definitely my inspiration.

===*one of the questions I never leave out of an interview is, as child what is the one thing you wanted to be*===

It is strange there is not really a lot of things I had on the list, I had wanted to be a nurse. I do not really like the sight of blood so that did not sit well with me, then this police idea came to mind.

===*what is your typical day like*===

Ok, I will take the difficult one, pollination period. I start at 07:30 and I go through my emails because I am the chairwoman of the WCBA, there are a lot of questions I have to answer sometimes. I will also look at the bees and check if everybody is doing their job. I would then get everything ready for the pollination process in terms of the number of hives, layout and so on. Then we would go and fetch bees from one farm and take them to the required area, by the time we finish it would be around 02:00 in the morning.

===*Lynette any words of wisdom or maybe advice you would give people that still find themselves in a corner in their career*===

I have always believed that what you really want sometimes it comes to you; do not shut your eyes and ears it will come to you. Find your passion and drive it till you get the best you want from it. Do not sit in the corner and say you do not know what to do; there is something for everybody to do.

--------------------------------**END**-----------------------

When I first met Lynette, it was purely work related. I was there to carry out some work for the company that employed me at the time. I was choosing a power-line route, which would go across their property. Now the route I had chosen meant that there would be trees that would need to be cut down for safety measures. When I presented the idea to her, she jumped up the minute I mentioned bush clearing and I knew right then that she was a nature lover. On my second visit to her house, I had to ask her what she did for a living. This happened around the time when I was deeply searching for a female entrepreneur that I would include in the book. As I explained to her what it is that I do, she quickly stopped me and started talking about passion, I knew right there she had to be in the book. I think in many instances we take things at face value and do not take time to figure out how things work and to me this was one of those cases. Bees were things I just slapped against the wall with a shoe when they came inside the house and that was it. There are a number of things that I never get to investigate, and I now know better.

I arrived at Lynette's office and found her waiting. One

thing I noticed outside was some renovation work-taking place and built on a veranda on to an existing house. What was interesting was how the veranda was constructed around an existing oak tree to avoid cutting it. Lynette mentions during the interview how her father would take her for trips to nature conservation areas when she was still young. Her love for nature goes a long way and she mentions that they are not running a business for the sake of making money, they love the bees and nature. I do believe that we are in business to make money and the love of what we are doing needs to be the only thing driving us, especially during the tough times. If there is no love or passion, we leave room for many things to come between the business and ourselves.

Going forward, Lynette also mentions that while growing up she wanted to be a nurse and I thought I should draw out the key values required for one to be a nurse and I found this on the internet:

- Care – This goes back to when she stopped me trying to protect the trees I was trying to have cut. She also mentions how bees will leave the hive when you do not care for them.
- Compassion – Before the interview, we had discussed the criminal activities that were taking place around the city and she sympathised with the victims.

- Competence – Lynette manages to bring out this skill in her attempt to climb up the ranks as a police officer. She also touches on how hard you have to work the ranks and to have the required experience.
- Courage – She shows courage from the start, choosing a career in the police. She also recalls a taxi violence incident and a hostage situation where she would have to make tough choices. In her current career as a beekeeper and travelling with bees, getting stung, that requires some courage to a certain extent.
- Commitment – she mentions during the interview that she just wanted to climb the ranks in the police, a course which she was very committed in achieving
- Communication – Lynette speaks about how she had to negotiate in a hostage situation and that on itself requires good communication skills.

I compared the caring for bees with a patient in a hospital where the nurse is not taking good care of them, they will at some point, consider leaving that hospital. This was also proof for me that we already know what we want to do as kids and hold the qualities; this just needs to be well cultivated.

CHAPTER FOUR

The Juggernauts

They'll tell you 'failure is not an option'. That is ridiculous, failure is always an option. Failure is the most readily available option at all times; but it's a choice. You can choose to fail or you can choose to succeed — Chael P. Sonnen

REUBEN RIFFEL OF REUBEN RESTAURANTS

INTRODUCTION: I first heard of Chef Reuben from my colleagues who watched the Season 3 Master Chef SA. I must admit I did not know why they went on the way they did about cooking, but something I soon picked up was his remarkable story of combining passion and determination.

===*Reuben I watched a video of you speaking about the challenges of Groendal, the township where you grew up on the Hope through Action website. You mentioned a number of interesting things on the video particularly the challenges of the community. Would say that the challenges facing the community have changed since your time growing up there and how*===

It is a great honour to be able to assist people and

organisations. There are amazing people out there helping others. My job is to bring awareness to these organisations and to help where i can with fund raising.

===*You became an ambassador of Hope Through Action, what does it mean for you personally*===

I think we all have our own set of values, standards and boundaries. It is all about managing those. It becomes very clear things are slacking once things are not synchronised with those values.

===*Reuben, you opened your first restaurant in the same town you grew up in and have hired locals as well, how did you find the experience*===

My focus was just to prevent the whole venture from failing initially. I did not necessarily have all the tools and knowledge, I just had my limited experience and those values I mentioned earlier to assist me. The locals that joined me mostly had pride in doing the job with me. Most businesses in Franschhoek do the same thing; the difference was that I progressed from being their colleague to being the guy that pays their salaries.

===*would you say that operating in the familiar grounds at first gave you an advantage over the competitors in terms of knowing the local market* ===

Yes, a little bit, but more so because I was working with people that I knew and that supported me.

===I read on some website that your taste for good food started when your mother would bring food from a restaurant she worked at. Do you still remember the feeling/emotion that came with taste of the food and have you tasted any better food since then===

I still remember that. Obviously, the enjoyment of food depends also on your state of mind and specific circumstances. Even though I have tasted better food since then, because that was my first introduction to gourmet style food I still rate it highly.

===one of your first jobs was working with your old man in the construction industry, how you would say you found the experience and what were the lessons learnt===

Well, I got more respect for my dad seeing what they had to do on a day-to-day basis. I learnt that people respect hard workers, but that they can also exploit that. The biggest lesson was that I definitely was not geared up to be a builder.

===at what age was this and how far did the schooling go===

I finished matric and the next year I started working with my dad.

===around about this time in your life, had you really managed to figure out what you wanted to do with your life as far as a career was concerned or you had planned to take anything that came along===

I did not know what I wanted to do, I wanted to go study but that was because some of my friends were also studying. I did not have something clear in mind. My mom threatened to kick me out if I did not make up my mind or started working.

===*and as a child, what was the one thing you wanted to be when you were old*===

I wanted to be a travel journalist or a teacher.

===*I am finding that mothers play a crucial role in most entrepreneurs' lives. I read on a website how your mother took you out of the construction industry and got you a job as a waiter. What do you think she saw in you at the time*===

Hahahaha!!! I think she just wanted me to earn some cash. The construction business is weather dependent and that meant lots of time at home when it rained.

===*Moving from construction to the restaurants industry sounds like quite a drastic change, how did you find this move and was it easy to adapt*===

Well, I was young and did not really get into the construction business wholeheartedly. It was an easy transition.

===*When you took the job as a waiter, do you think you had something planned? I am thinking of being a restaurant manager or slowly disappear to being behind the scenes*===

For me, I saw it temporal until I could figure out what I wanted in life, or what I wanted to be.

===*you soon moved from being a waiter to the kitchen. What motivated this move and perhaps share what you think your employer saw in you at the time*===

Again, more necessity that anything else; also maybe fate played a role. They were short staffed in the kitchen, I was maybe the worst waiter, but willing and able, so they chose me.

===*what do you remember the most about your early days in the kitchen*===

Tasting so many things, learning and for the first time feeling like I was part of a team. Doing service in a restaurant is like a live show. When service starts, the curtain goes up and everything has to run like clockwork. After service once compliments are received it's a great feeling to have been part of something successful.

===*you had a mentor Richard Carstens. In your view what is a mentor and what role do they play*===

A mentor understands you and introduces you to the reality of the job and then teaches you the ropes, I learned the ropes by watching more than through proper tutoring.

===*while working at Chamonix, you found yourself having to take over Richard's role. How did you find this and was there any fear of having to fit in his shoes===*

Yes off course, this person was and still is one of our best chefs. Many that have taken over from him have failed. I had a lot of support though, from my fellow chefs.

===by this stage, did you know where you were heading in terms of your career, perhaps elaborate a bit on your plan===

Well, I finally realized that this is the job for me; I felt I was good at it and I wanted to learn more. I was offered jobs all over and my aim then was to work with more chefs around the country to learn as much as possible from them.

===you moved over to the next job, what motivated the move ===

I met some people that were traveling around South Africa; they had lunch with me and offered me a job. These type of things happened frequently, I had a job lined up as well in the Middle East, but declined that to go to the UK.

===When one is married, moving around is not always an easy thing to do. Would you say having a supportive partner helps in terms of being flexible to move when the opportunity presents itself===

Yes, especially early on in your career and maybe better

if you do not have any kids. We were young and we had an appetite to travel and to explore. It was the coolest thing to be able to set up shop overseas.

===*One of the things we believe in at Frist Idea is the ability and skill to put together the information that we collect. While you were in Cambridge, your construction skill came in handy, can you share with us what happened*===

Well as the world sometimes work, people promise a lot and cannot always deliver. Once I got to the promised restaurant, it was so far from completion, that I felt I needed to step in and help move things forward. I helped with the roof construction, flooring, painting and tiling. Initially, we thought of going back home but I think I made the right decision at the time.

===*I think most of us when we are offered a job, we will only be willing to do what we were hired for, what made you rise to the occasion and go that extra mile*===

I met the builders at that stage and could see this was going to take long. I was keen to get cooking and was lucky to have worked in construction. If everything in life always goes to plan it would be a perfect world, but it is not and we get tested regularly in life. Shifting things along to others will get you nowhere. I did blame the owner for not being on top of this from the beginning, but that was not going to solve the problem.

===*some decisions we are forced into, others we say yes to the one thing and then a lot good come things come with. I believe friends offered you the opportunity to start your own restaurant, was this all in good timing===*

I felt at the time I wanted to continue in England, when this offer came through I had the opportunity to take over this restaurant, but instead decided to come home. It was great timing yes. I have always felt that I have made good decisions although you also make bad ones.

===often when one starts a new business you find a number of things that go wrong before launching. This can be something as small as a light bulb or equipment not delivered on time. Did you have anything similar to this happening and how did you deal with it===

Many things can go wrong. You always start with the fairy-tale and quickly get brought down to reality. We were overseeing many things from the kitchen layout, equipment as well as working with the designers etc. I remember we opened close to winter and our fireplace was smoking badly the first couple of evenings. That caused a bit of havoc.

===normally with new ventures people want to start something today and be sitting on top of the world by next weekend. You started humbly from being a waiter, how has this helped you in how you deal with your employees today==

I know what it is like to be in their shoes. We never achieve perfection, we never get to that success it's ever illusive. I believe respect is important, we can work hard, and I can be straight about an issue without having to disrespect my staff. We are a team and we always strive to give people that perspective.

===*your name fitted in quite well with the naming of the company... What significance does naming a company hold to you*===

It is important, but a name becomes what your business and your style is. The aura around the name is created long after the name is chosen.

===*you expanded to other areas as well, what you look for when you plan to open a new place*===

I prefer towns that I have a connection with, also if I feel we can bring something different to the restaurant landscape then I am all for it.

===*when we start a business, we are sometimes not aware of all the possibilities. You have published a few books and do training as well, what other things does the company do*===

We are involved in outside catering, consulting, endorsements and TV

===*you were fortunate enough to find something you love and passionate about at a young age, what do you think is key for achieve this*===

It is important to get out there and to develop your

interests. If you are willing to work hard, and at times to be a fly on the wall, it gives you a lot of insight. The rest is straight forward, hard work and constantly take stock of where you are, who you have become and where you want to be.

===*On your website, I found the following* **OFTEN WE DON'T EVEN REALISE THAT MANY OF OUR PREFERENCES IN LATER LIFE - SHAPES, COLOURS TASTES - COME FROM THINGS WE LOVED AS CHILDREN** – *Do you think this was the case with you as well*===

Well yes, I grew up in a family that loved cooking and eating. We lived close with nature in the way that our food was produced and utilised.

===*what is the most valuable lesson you learnt on your journey*===

Never burn bridges, stay true to yourself, and be proud of where you come from.

===*any advice for upcoming guys in the game*===

It is important not to get caught up in the hype of things. Today everything is fast tracked and everyone seems to know it all. Knowledge and information is nothing if it cannot be applied meaningfully. Learn from people around you and always respect people around you. Listen to your gut and remember that success cannot come without sacrifices and hard work.

===*can you take me through your typical workday from when you get up till the end of day*===

I get up and check mails. Go to work, have breakfast. Plan our day with my chefs. My wife runs my diary so I have to sit with her and yay or nay. Talk to all our people in the other restaurants, sometimes travel there. Talk to suppliers and attend various meetings. If I am lucky, I get to cook some food. Come home spend time with my kids and then back to work until 23:00, watch some TV and sleep.

------------------------------END------------------------

At the time of the interview, Reuben's diary was quite full so the interview had to be conducted via email. I had been to Franschoek, a number of times before, knew it as one of the towns in the country that was rich with history. I never knew any specific area in the town itself and I saw this as an opportunity to visit one of Reuben's Restaurants. I wanted to experience the culture and atmosphere in the restaurants and some of the workers quickly welcomed me. As I waited for my lunch, I was browsing around trying to get a feel of the restaurant. I came across some of Reuben's cooking books and also came across a Kitchen Aid store which I learnt was also run by Reuben. These were all things I was not aware about before the interview. My thoughts at the time were more about how one business could have so many potentials; it did not just end at the cooking. Reuben also does a number of ads on TV; he was one of the judges on Master Chef SA. Before the interview, I was chatting to a former colleague who had shared how Reuben had helped in his niece's school and later found that he was involved in a number of community projects. On one video, he mentions a number of times how he likes to be part of something that is successful and this has echoed a number of times in my head ever since I listened to that clip. It is evident in his business how this holds value to him. This goes back to also when he took over from his mentor and also revealed again when he was in the UK and made sure that the restaurant was opened on time. If we could take out any one of those, there is a huge chance that he might not be where he is today. There are many who would refuse to take such a path without weighing the potential opportunities. I think more importantly, what I learnt was that we have to start somewhere and work our way with an open mind to possibilities. It was a true story of hard work and dedication paying off.

VICTOR. ZWANE OF DELACOM SOLUTIONS

INTRODUCTION: Growing up in my hometown I used to see Victor around the dusty streets, I will be referring to him as Delane. He was a couple of years my senior and soon disappeared from the town after he matriculated. He surfaced a number of years later and the word was at the time he was working for the National Lottery. A few years later, I learnt that he had started his own company. I have occasionally met him at some events around the town and on very few occasions had a beer with him. One of the things I can recall from my previous chats with him was how he struggled with partners when he was starting his business.

===*Delane I have known you for some time, but hold no background info, can you just give a bit of background on yourself in terms of where you grew up and where did you go to study*===

Chief I was born in 1977 in Kwazulu Natal in a township called Ntuzuma. In the mid-1980s, I moved to Cala and that is where I grew up. This is where I did my primary school up to the high school level until 1997. I moved to PE around 1998 and I went to a technical college to do my electrical engineering, which took +/- 3years.

===*can you share what you wanted to be when you grew up?*===

The reason why I ask this is that I have wanted to be many things in my short life from a doctor, teacher, and an astronaut at one point===

Because of the area, we grew up in, as you would also know, there were what we called administrators just to cut it short, teachers, police, and magistrates. Being a doctor was just a privilege at the time, but I was interested in becoming umtshutshisi (a prosecutor). During my spare time, I would even go to court just to listen to how they conducted the court cases, that was my interest.

===that is one of the things that I picked up from a previous interview that people who grew up in areas like Cala were very limited in terms of the different career paths they could take back then, but fortunately times are changing and we are able to see things better today. Can you explain to us what is that Delacom Solutions does===

Delacom's core business is electrical, focusing on electrical work. We specialise in maintenance for wastewater treatment, especially for the Municipality and we are also involved in construction. We have also undertaken some investments in property, but not at a large scale. We have also developed another company under Delacom called Bayethe, which deals with mechanical engineering.

===*I see it has been a while since we last chatted, that is quite a lot of development since then. What is your role in the company*==

I would say I am a Project Director because I am directly involved with projects. I also play a role of a Business Developer whereby I go out and try to get business for the company. Once I secure work for the company, I play the project director role where I work together with my electrician to do development planning and implementation of the project until it gets to the final stages. So I would say I play two roles.

===*going back, would you say that you have always wanted to be involved in business Delane, or was it something you picked up along the way and fell in love with? And if that was the case, what would you say you wanted to do*===

Ok, I think since I grew up in an environment whereby my mom, Sis Phumla sold secrets socks, pork, and shoes, during that time I learnt how to deal with people. When you deal with people, you have to know how to communicate with them. This is where I realised that this is a way to generate income and while I was helping my mom out, I also had my own business running on the side. I realised that income is not about one's salary, you can survive through running a business. This is not something I was interested in; with time, I fell in love with the process as the time went.

When I started Delacom, it was much easier for me as there was no difference between the process of selling secret socks and going to negotiate a deal with a public servant from the department of public works. The attitude is the same and the approach is the same as going from door to door selling shoes. Sometimes people feel that when you talk about big companies like Transnet, the stakes change because of the name, in the end you are dealing with people. That is one of the things I learnt, forget about Transnet and say ok, I am dealing with Litha Ndabula now; I understand he works for Transnet. When I measure my approach now, it is almost the same as then and that is how I operate.

===*that is one of the key things that can limit one. Especially someone like myself, we see these big company names and say No, no, no, that's definitely a no go zone. And talking about falling in love with the processes, most people end up doing things they do not love and I think this does put some kind of strain on a person later on. You know when we dream of our businesses we see everything in a straight line. We tend to think that toady we are staying in Motherwell and by teatime tomorrow, we will be staying in Sandton in Jozi. Would you say you saw a straight line when you started out===*

Let me give you a little background on Delacom. My first job was at VW where I was a material controller working for a logistics company. I had tried by all means, to get to a better position, but later got an offer from the National Lottery. They took me to Johannesburg for 2months training on how to deal with their network. Now as I travelled with National Lottery, I started meeting different people from different areas around the country. I realized that there are a lot of opportunities out there and people were not aware of this. Fortunately, my boss also pushed me to become an entrepreneur. Our operations then with Lotto were structured as follows; we had the retailer, we had two teams that included electrical and network technicians. We carried out work as far as George and Colesburg. The company used to absorb the costs of two trips to site when going to do installations. Bear in mind that I have an electrical engineering background, but now doing networks which is mainly for IT technicians. While I was interacting with my boss, I came up with the proposal that I wanted to have my own small company that will do electrical installations. The plan was to use the company vehicle with my electrician to go and do installations. The result was that the company managed to save on costs. This is where I opened the doors for myself. I then went to an organisation called Umsobovu who had appointed a consultant and I found that the consultant was an old white man who was an engineer. He also became my mentor and guided me to acquire a big project from the Municipality for wastewater treatment. Since then it has been kind of smooth sailing.

===*speaking about mentors, would you recommend that a person starting out should have a mentor and was that helpful in your case*===

It was very helpful as he was really a good mentor to me. You know sometimes I thought the guy was against me or had a problem with me. He was harsh towards me and he trained me as if I was in a military camp. I now know that during operations there is no love in business. When things are harsh, you have to be also harsh be it dealing with your employees or clients. That experience with my boss being harsh, it taught me to be strong. On certain occasions when you are negotiating a deal, you have to be harsh, because we are talking about money and sometimes you have to put your foot down. Looking back, I thought my boss was being funny, now I know he was only training me to be ready for the market. He told me that out there it would be quite different to what I am used to.

===*I liked what you mentioned earlier about your ability to see and implement a cost saving process for your boss and I am sure that the skill has helped you as well in your business. We hear people talking about getting out of your comfort zone. It does not always work for everyone, but do you personally believe this worked for you*===

Before I resigned from Lotto, my business was already operating. I had received an offer from Transnet; they had wanted to train me to become an artisan. The offer was much more than the salary I was already getting. I took a decision, which was between me working for Transnet or for my own company, and as you also know, it is not easy to get to work for these big companies. When I made the decision, I knew that if I rejected the offer, Transnet would hire someone else, but I would go out there and hire 5 or 10 people. It was not easy for me to make it because Transnet offered housing allowance, medical aid and other things.

===*When as the company formed*===

2005

===*talking about the founding stages, did you have any partners or was it just you*===

Because it is an electrical company, we started out as four guys. One was from UCT and the others I went to school with. The others were all more qualified than I was, but not all of us can become entrepreneurs. One of the things I learnt is that you should not run a business because you have a qualification as maybe an artisan or an engineer that is very dangerous. This is what I picked up from these guys, they were not interested in what I was trying to do. I negotiated with each of them and they ended up resigning, all three of them. I went back to my mentor and told him that all my stakeholders have resigned and I was interested in their skill. He organised a guy who was a master electrician and he was running his own business. He was not an entrepreneur; he was an electrician running a business. He had the skill, but not the skill needed to unlock the market. We worked together for about 2-3 years and he was a silent partner, but due to certain problems, he resigned. So overall, Delacom has had five directors in the past, I remain the only one now.

===*I can imagine that must have been quite tough. When we look at the company name, it is something that is important and must not really restrict you. I am imagining a scenario where you would find a company called Fried Chicken; you step inside only to find it is a gymnasium. I mentioned earlier that we grew up calling you Delane, could this have anything to do with the name Delacom Solutions*===

Yes. Dela is from Delane and Com is from communications since I was involved in communications while working for Lotto. I did not want the company to focus on the communication side only because my first deal was for communication and electrical. At the same time my decision was not about what I could do now, it was about targeting what I could do in the industry.

===*seemingly, that was a wise move and people tend to get that wrong. You chose to operate in PE, I mean there must have been at least 100 other companies you were going to compete with. Can you share with us the thinking behind this decision? Someone else for example would have decided to go and operate in the rural area than compete in the city===*

If you remember 2005, Coega was at a development stage. Secondly, as I mentioned before that I was already working for the national lottery in PE. It was based on the availability of work, development and the amount of research I had done by then. If you remember, the term BEE came around that time, that if you were a black person you would benefit in some of the work. I used that to my advantage at the time.

===opportunities are what we need to look out for wherever they are. Looking at your competitors then and now, would you say it has become easier to compete over the years in the industry===

To be honest, in this industry, there is no competition. As I told you before we started the interview, t I am involved in wastewater treatment and I am still the only black person operating within that field; there is not much competition. My only competitors are mostly white owned companies whereby the current government policies are also in my favor when I bid with them. I do not want to say I only get awarded work because of my skin colour, I am getting work because of my experience. I do use the advantage though. Especially now that there is the CIDB program, do you know what that is?

===*No, please explain*===

Ok, it's a program that is being run by the government and how it works is that if you complete a project that's worth more than 500k, your get rated higher and it's only a few of us who qualify for this; so the chances of me getting work have increased. For the past 2years or so most of the work that I am getting, is mostly clients that are coming to me. I do apologise, I do not mention this to brag, but I do not go out looking for work, the work comes to me. As I told, you that Coega called me about a project worth R13million, which I am currently busy on. I was not even aware of the project. The projects that I am currently running in the former Transkei it is all calls I get that there is a project at a certain place, are you interested? I think this is also because the company will be turning 10years next year (2015), so I think that it is because of my reputation in the industry. The quality of work is really, what has worked for me.

===*Wow 10years that is quite a milestone there. If we look at what I call the "cloud of doubt" which is basically that stage where one is very uncertain at the start of the company. Sometimes you even feel like quitting, would you say you have experienced such.* ===

I would say no. Whatever challenges I had, I found my strength in the name Delacom because that represents me. I had no choice; I had to keep this thing alive. I have a policy that says if there is a problem, there is a solution and it really works for me. The only challenges I learnt from is that partnership does not really work at a small scale. You can be a partner with your sister, brother or friend, in a small company this does not really work. I think it has something to do with our background. Our mentality has been affected by poverty and I am not talking about starving for food. I am referring to the lack of knowledge and when the doors were opened, everyone wanted to have money, greed took over. From my experience is that partnership does not work period, it is better to have a joint venture.

===*you mentioned something about how your clients keep coming back to you. What would say it that one thing that makes them to keep coming back to you*===

It is the quality of work, communication and the marketing strategy that I make use of. Of all the projects, I have undertaken, I have never been late; and I always delivered on time. Yes, there are challenges at times, but I go through them. I meet the legal requirements and I have built good resources within the company.

===definitely agree with the quality of work being very crucial. We see quite a number of companies undertaking projects they cannot complete. I think the main cause of this problem is that people are chasing money before quality as you mentioned earlier. What are the staff numbers looking like now? Knowing very well that it is not always possible to keep employees happy, what is your advice on this===

As you had mentioned that it is not always possible to keep everyone happy, people have different backgrounds and have different ways of thinking. I do try to interact with my staff on a ground level and I am currently sitting with about 60 employees. It is difficult to get to every one of them, but to keep them happy you must try to understand their background. You need to be there for them when things are tough, especially when they are stuck on projects. You need to try to come up with solutions and not run away from them. This is how you start earning their support.

===getting to the funding, what were your challenges around the matter? Did you find that it was easily accessible and what advice would you give to upcoming entrepreneurs===

When it comes to funding, you must learn to start on a small scale. The reason is that you still need to learn the ins and outs. You will be shocked that some are awarded jobs of up to R2million and do not know what a cheque book or UIF is. You have to start small and I told myself that I am in a college for 5years not academically, but in terms of practicality. I started on a small scale with no loan only making use of my salary. I had a small personal loan just to buy the little things like a fax machine and so on. I then build up my record with the bank, the bank is not about what you have, and it is about what is in and what is out. You gain points by doing that and I learnt that builds you a record with the bank. Because I was doing electrical work, I used the advantage of suppliers and creditors whereby if I buy something I would pay them after 60days. I could say I never really applied for a loan at the start; I did however get a business overdraft due to the growth of the business.

===*what do you think that the financial institutions could do to make things better for someone who is starting out*===

The people who are assisting us are mostly women and do not really have a background of the business environment. They do not really understand the pain you have to go through. Personally, I think they should employ people who know and understand what the client's needs are.

===*As a business owner, I am assuming that there were terms like profit margins and expenses that you eventually had to know. Would you say you had a bit of background of these terms, read books or started to communicate with people who were directly involved with them?===*

I worked through my accountant and was able to learn all the accounting terms. We were really interacting with each other a lot.

===Getting to the expansion stages, at FIRST IDEA we believe that it is always that first business idea that will eventually open the window of opportunity to other ideas. Unfortunately, a lot depends upon what that first idea really is. You mentioned earlier that you started working with networks, electrical and now you are involved in mechanical engineering. I understand that you have also invested in property, can you share with us why Delacom decided to be a player in the property market===

Well you can see on my business card that there is electrical services and project management. What we are trying to take is a direction of project management in most sectors, although it is not possible to be involved in all sectors. The reason I entered into the property market was that the company was getting positive sales. I then asked myself that since I have X-amount of cash what can I do with it. What happens if I cannot secure anything in the future and how will I survive? I took a decision to invest in property so that when things are sour from the project side, I would still be able to generate income from the property side. It was mainly to have fixed assets and I used to say

"Inkomozam" (my herd of cattle). Honestly speaking our age group is used to and still makes silly decisions in terms of spending what we have. The move into property was based on securing what I had worked for the last 4-5 years.

===*that is a very interesting take there because we find that most people will rather go and buy five or ten cars. Before we started the interview, you mentioned that you do not have your own house; you are waiting to buy in the right area when the time comes. Can you share this with us*===

I was interested in the bank-repossessed properties and I secured my own in Motherwell where the selling price of the area was between R300 000 and R400 000. What I have done is that I managed to get a bond for that house which was on auction at R130 000, I will disclose my figures. Then my interest in property grew and I went back to the bank to get a second bond. When I got that second bond, I went to the auction again and I secured a property, which was not attached to the bond, but I utilised the bond funds. Therefore, if something happened to the first property, it would not affect the second one. This is where I figured that there is a gap in the property industry. I then took a decision to move from the township to the urban zone due to security reasons. I was involved a lot in local projects and dealing with the local community in terms of general labourers and other stuff. It was based on my security, and to be in the central zone. For example, the offices and the airport are about a 5-minute drive from my residence.

===*if you could take us through things like the property and business cycle, what would you say one must look out for? I made an example earlier about how a club owner might be affected by sin tax, month ends and so on. In your line of things like government, spending comes into mind for me*===

You know what, there is something that we are forgetting; maybe we are just ignorant about it. South Africa is currently in a development stage, amongst other countries like Brazil if I am correct. For the next 30years, South Africa will be busy. The problem is how we conduct ourselves as entrepreneurs. One of the mistakes we make is that we become arrogant in a sense that when we know how to secure a deal, we think we know everything. My experience is that when you start a business you need to have a junior bookkeeper and do things according to records. What I have learnt in the past 10years is to have an in-house junior accountant to record the ins and outs of the business. The reason why I mention this is that it had a negative impact when it came to the legal requirements in terms of tax clearance certificate. I recently had to pay close to R1million to SARS just to get a tax clearance certificate. The accountant is an end user and by the time you get to them, you have already taken a number of decisions. They compile what you bring in and submit it. Yes, I still do take silly decisions at times whereby the decision is based on the fact that the funds are available. Maybe, as the owner of the business one could look at going to do a junior bookkeeping course. Other will people will run away from banking, but by banking, you build points with your bank. When something big comes along and you need the bank, the bank will look at your financials and you could qualify for financing. For example one of the flats I bought in Joburg, I qualified 100% for a home loan and did not have to pay for costs. Currently now the property pays for itself. I even tell my colleagues that one day you will need a van and you will not be able to purchase it because you are running away from the bank.

===*would you say that there are certain times of the year where there is no work, perhaps things that one needs to look out for every year like Easter Holiday, Christmas in the case of a shop*===

In order to run away from such things you need to know and understand the cycle of your business. For example, I know that the Municipality's year-end is June. I know that things will be slow now and then next year around February; they will start dishing out a lot of work to meet their expenditure targets. It does not affect me much because I have studied my sector and I would advise people in other sectors to study theirs.

===*Delane, let us get to the marketing. How do you go about this and what platforms do you use*===

I make use of business cards, a company profile that I am currently circulating. I was in a position to start a Facebook group, as you also know that some people that we went to school with, might be working for the bigger companies. It could be someone I shared a desk with in school and they are maybe looking for a reputable company to employ. I also make use of newspapers and also subscribe to be updated about open tenders.

===*can you share what your typical work day is like*===

Ok at 05:00, I do light exercising and then I develop a programme for the day. I then check emails, I have two central emails where I review the last 2 to 3 days and see what has not been done yet. I then develop a daily programme from that. Right now, we have an office group on WhatsApp where I communicate the programme. The guys will then give me feedback on what has been done and what needs to be done. For the past two weeks, I have been busy trying to implement that.

===*surely that must help a lot to improve the communication in the office. What would you say you enjoy the most about your job now===*

To be under pressure, I like to be under pressure, but it does come with consequences. I do not like to seat in front of a PC, I am not a computer person. I prefer to give instructions and delegate. I like to come up with solutions where there are problems and this can be either technical or otherwise. My strategy is as follows; I let my employees enter the pot and when there are challenges, they call me. If you enter with them in the pot, you will be stressed, frustrated and you will not be able to apply a clear mind. It works for me to leave them alone and only come when they need me.

===that is some valuable input there and I am sure many people will find that valuable. What would you say are the negative things affecting the industry now? For example we read about bribery and corruption on the news===

Let me just be with honest with you, I am a man of solutions and I am fighting the negatives. From my side there is nothing negative and if there is a problem, it normally created by an individual who makes a silly decision. When someone creates such a case, you need to have a formula that works against such. To make an example when I had to get my tax clearance certificate, I had no choice, but to release my properties to get it. To be honest, my policy does not allow me room for negatives; if there is a problem, there is a solution.

Even if I can receive a call now, I have to make sure that I come up with a solution. I do understand that some problems will be worse than I anticipated.

===*you mentioned earlier that South Africa is in a development stage, where do you see the industry in the next 10 to 20 years? You have mentioned quite a number of things like the waste water treatment and development into Africa*===

If you look at where we are coming from in Cala, how it was in 1998, you moved to Cape Town, how has it changed now. What does that tell you about where we are going to in the next five to ten years? So now, why do you not participate in this change, be part of it then? A group of people creates change, why then do you not become part of that group. Yes, there will be always be challenges, why are you scared to come up with proposals? South Africa is growing and we should use that to our advantage. I would say we are blessed in South Africa. If you look at the retail industry in the townships, it has been taken over by foreign nationals, where are South African people? You can even look at the barbershops, restaurants; we have foreign nationals working there. We have the problem of not wanting to participate and I for one am not proud to say I am the only black person doing ABCD. It is not a good practise, what if something happens to me and I am no longer there. How long will it take to fill that gap again? There is a lot of ground we need to cover Chief.

===*I am starting to get the picture of what you are saying there. You find that companies from China are coming to Africa to invest while we as locals do not make use of this opportunity. As we sit here at the airport today, Delane is on his way to attend a course in Joburg. Delane, are the any books, website, conference you would recommend one attends*===

I have recently joined the Nelson Mandela Bay Business Chamber. It is a group of businesses from big to small where we meet and network. I am going to use the platform to get an understanding of how other entrepreneurs think. I have been offered a position on the board under the strategic panel in charge of developments around Nelson Mandela Bay. One question I had asked them was that they are trying to get all the investors to come and invest in South Africa, but do they have a maintenance programme to the existing infrastructure? They responded that it is with the municipality and I told them that there is nothing of a kind in place. I had to ask them then why did they run these concurrently then? There are also a number of programmes on TV and radio people can listen to. DjSbu from Metro FM has also been running a show on radio for the past 3 months. I would advise people to look up workshops and events in their areas. They do not have to talk; they can just listen, absorb information and then go do their own research. When I started my business I had the positive mentality that I will get projects, my tune has now changed. I am looking now looking for people to work with and can transparently say this is what I am bringing to the table, what do you have to offer? I would not do something like that before, but you would be surprised how people would turn down something like that.

===*Delane if we could take one thing and one thing only that stood out for you since starting your company till now, what would it be*===

It has been meeting different people with different attitudes. A man I had an interview with once said there are people who are dishonest and those who are honest. If you collect that information there will be always be something positive to learn. I have been very honest in this interview, maybe the next person will not honest. You will have to decide what you take from it.

----------------------------END----------------------------

I arrived in Port Elizabeth in the morning, 2hours before the scheduled interview. I could not help but take advantage of that and spend the little time I had walking on the beach. My journey does not end in PE for the day; I had made plans to be in Cape Town by evening. I spent little time worrying about the interview or whether it will start on time. The interview is to take place at the airport. Delane arrives 10minutes before the scheduled time and I find myself relieved that he showed up early. He informs that he will be catching a flight to Johannesburg in just under 4hours and once again, I was impressed by how he managed to be punctual. We spent about an hour chatting about business in general. The interview began sharply at 11 o'clock after he looked at his watch. I was so caught up in the conversation we were having that I lost track of time and not realizing that an hour had passed. Once again, I am impressed by his proficiency of *time management*. What strikes me from the beginning is that he mentions he was interested in being a prosecutor when he was still young. He goes further and mentions how he would spend time *listening to* court cases when he was young. He mentions the word **listen** for the first time. Later his advice to people is to attend events in their areas and just take the time to **listen.** He learnt how to *communicate and negotiate* at a young age, I also make note of how he manages to simplify this to selling secrets socks for his mother. He does not choose a complicated analogy that needs a formula to work out and due to this kind of thinking, he is able to look at an individual of a company and not what company the individual works for. I think I would tremble when I hear that I will be dealing with a big company. He ends off by saying: *"When I measure my approach now, it's almost the same as then and that is how I operate."* This skill, he carries with him and by measure. He again mentions how he had to negotiate with all his stakeholders to resign from the company. What stands out again was his attempt to **cut costs** for his former boss by doing both electrical and network installations. From my personal experience when I work for a company, that would really be the last thing I look at. He managed to use this opportunity to negotiate a deal that would not only benefit the company, but himself as well.

He also makes note of how his former boss trained him as if he was in a military camp, but he is now able to see where this ties up with his work now. Self-confidence forms an important part of any entrepreneur and Delane very boldly states that if he rejected the offer from Transnet, someone else would be offered the job. He would not only reject the job, but was determined that he will go out there and hire 5 to 10 people. At first, I could not understand when he spoke about the dangers of opening a business just because you have a qualification in that field. Statistics as it stands in the year 2014; the number of billionaires with no varsity qualification is three times the number of those with qualifications. I guess to a certain extent, this justifies what he said. Qualified individuals open companies in the field that they qualified in, only because of the level of safety that comes with. We are taught in many ways to memorise and replicate and since many law firms have been opened before, there is that sense of security that it is okay to open your own and fail. The naming of the company holds significant meaning to him. He boldly states that the name Dela is his name, he had to make the company survive, and it represents him. A bit later, he reiterates this by saying; *"Whatever challenges I had, I found my strength in the name Delacom because that is me."* I am made aware of his vision for the company when he makes this point. He also makes us aware of how he saw his partners were not interested in what he was trying to do. In most cases, we need to review this with our partners and staff members as well. If they do not share your vision of the company, maybe we are to consider looking for people who will. The vision is also revealed when he says they would like to be involved in a number of sectors, particularly the project management.

"If there is a **problem**, *there is a solution."* From almost the beginning of Delacom, this is portrayed by his cost cutting strategy for his boss. I learnt of how he had to negotiate with his stakeholders to resign. The problem was the difference in the vision they had for the company. Around this point we also see how the "military camp" (harsh treatment) from his former boss pays off.

To get his tax clearance certificate, he had to sell some of his properties. He referred to his properties as "IinkomoZam"; this tells me that they had a significant value to him. Yet, he is able to release them to solve the current problem he is faced with. I also review how he brought up the maintenance of the current infrastructure, the problem solving skill continue to show. Going further, I start to analyse how he keeps his eyes open looking for gaps to operate in. Although he mentions that he is still the only black person doing the type of work he does, he is not proud of this. He has been able to utilise this advantage even when he started out in 2005. Another approach is how he bought one property on auction and went to buy another one utilising the funds of the first one. Twice during the interview, he talks about research. Personally, I think we live in an age where access to information is much easier than ever before.

Frugality in economics refers to prudent planning in the disposition of resources to avoid unnecessary waste or expense. At the time when his business was booming, he did not waste money, but tried to build security for worse times. Capital preservation remains key for most entrepreneurs and remaining self-employed has to be the top priority. When we get to **managing employees** he acknowledges that it is not possible to keep all staff happy. The important thing I have learnt when it comes to employees is that you have to stick with the winners, those are the people that will take you in the right direction. He mentions how it is important to understand your employee's background. It just so happened that before the interview we touched on this and I was sharing about an employee I recently hired. He asked if this particular employee has a driver's licence and I replied that I am actually trying to assist him towards getting one. He then mentioned that even if he later decides to leave the company, he would not have wasted time working for me. Yes one needs to manage the time people come to work, manage the output and while doing that maybe one should also looking at understanding the needs of their employees; after all these are the people that you depend on for your income to a certain extent.

Towards the end, he speaks of how Cala was in 1998; most people will not know this. To give them a slight background: *Imagine a small town; the main road is a very bad dirt road. There are no franchises, no big supermarket, no descent filling station, etc. The only businesses in town are shops owned by a number of locals, the kind of shops where you buy over the counter. There were no banks, ATMs around, locals have travel had to drive 31 km to have access to these. The local hospital did not even have descent parking, let alone enough rooms. The kind of town you could do 120 km/h driving through the main road with no speed humps, stop streets or traffic circles.*

Sixteen years later, a few things have changed; the main road is tarred, there are two banks operating in town, three big supermarkets, a handful of franchise stores, shopping complex, a new hospital.

These developments must have cost hundreds of millions. These were changes that were brought about by people like you and me. Delane asks, why do you not participate in this change and be part of it?

In my summary, I highlighted a number of things and

some might be wondering why. To refresh our minds these were *time management, listening, learning, communication, negotiating, cost saving, problem, managing employees*

I visited www.mymajors.com, which is a website that helps people choose their careers paths and what skills are needed for that career.

I looked up Prosecutor and this is what I found:

- Time Management - Managing one's own time and the time of others.

- Active Listening - Giving full attention to what other people are saying, taking time to understand the points being made, asking questions as appropriate

- Complex Problem Solving - Identifying complex problems and reviewing related information to develop and evaluate options and implement solutions.

- Judgment and Decision Making - Considering the relative costs and benefits of potential actions to choose the most appropriate one.

- Negotiation - Bringing others together and trying to reconcile differences.

GREG HEASLEY OF NAKED PENGUIN BOY

INTRODUCTION: I must say I was lucky to bump into Greg sometime early in 2013 on a visit to Cape Town. We would often joke around until one day I overheard him chatting to someone about his job as a Stipendiary Steward. That did not make sense to me then, however I made an effort to find out what he was doing these days.

===*Greg, I recently learnt that you have not had a CV for the past 13years, how so*===

In June 2001, after trying my hand at varying types of jobs/careers, my brothers and I got together and we discussed the setting up of our own business. I have not had the need for a CV since then fortunately.

===*you have worked in quite a number of places and in different industries if I may add. Was that always part of the plan*===

I do not think I actually had a plan. The majority of my jobs were while I was travelling, so I would take whatever I could, as money was always tight.

===*can you take me through your early life in terms of where you were born and studied*===

I was born in Durban, South Africa. I went to Queensburgh Boys High School and then onto College to study Mechanical Engineering.

===*as kids we often have dreams of different career paths we wanted to follow, what would you say yours was* ===

I always wanted to be involved in the Horse Racing industry. It happened for me.

===*what happened to it*===

It happened for me. Horses and horseracing have been my passion since I was a kid and I was fortunate enough to work in the industry for several years.

===*I am going to ask something I do not usually ask, looking back at your years in school, what did you excel in*===

I do not think I excelled in anything really. I was always in the top quarter, so I did alright.

===*Greg, at what age did you start working and why*===

I started working when I was about 16. I was a Jockeys Agent, working from my bedroom or at the races after school (normally).

===*you were in school at that time still, how did you cope*===

When you find something in life that you are absolutely passionate about, it does not seem like work, you're making big decisions for the Jockey you represent and for your own reputation. I was doing something that I loved doing, so I would be studying the horses every spare moment I had.

===*would you say that by the time you were in high school you knew what you wanted to do with your life*===

Difficult one, I knew that I wanted to be involved in the Horse Racing industry; I knew that ultimately I wanted to become a Stipendiary Steward. At the same time, I always saw myself owning my own business.

===*you also sold cool drinks at the racecourse, did you find interacting with people easy* ===

I was young and confident; it was fun days.

===*would you say you learnt anything from that*===

I learnt that no matter how long you have the cool drinks in that fridge for, they are never cold enough for the customer.

===*you went from selling cool drinks to being a jockey agent. Please explain what does a jockey agent do and perhaps how you got the job*===

It was when I was selling cool drinks at the races, I overheard a conversation that there was a certain jockey that was looking for an agent. I just jumped over the counter and went straight to the Jockey's Room. I am still not sure how I got through security. I got to speak to the Jockey for a few minutes and I started.

A jockey's agent does all the booking of rides for the Jockey. So, about 2 weeks before the race you're already phoning the trainers or owners to see if the jockey you're representing can ride their horse. It takes a great deal of racing knowledge to do a successful job.

===*had the thought of becoming a jockey agent ever crossed your mind before then*===

It did actually, I used to see the agents at the races talking to all the trainers and owners, and you had to be a very sociable person.

===*and school, how far did that go*===

I left in Standard 8 to go to College. I thought I knew better than everyone did at the time. Kids – Stay at school!

===*"Go to school, Get a degree, Get a good job and Get a career… What would you say your view of this was back then*===

I was not too worried about planning very much, I was always confident that something would work out for me. I just wanted to be independent and start working.

===*and now*===

I am already putting the cash away for my daughters to go to University.

===*Most young white males had to do a bit of service those days in the army, did you suffer the same fate*===

Yes, I was sent off to Potchefstroom, did a Junior Leader's course that got me the rank of a Bombadier. I was there last year for compulsory National service.

===*within a year in the army you were already training new recruits that seems like quite good progress*===

My Junior Leader's course was 3 months of hell. It was after that, that I was ready to start training new recruits.

===*you later jetted off to London, how did this happen*===

I always wanted to travel a bit before getting all serious again in business.

===*people hold on to culture, history and their origin. Heck, I do too. The thought of leaving home scares me. Was this easy for you*===

It was easy for me, I love London, I wanted a family and SA at the time did not seem the safest place to bring them up.

===*did you have a job secured in London or at least know people there*===

My cousin was there, it was in the East end of London. There were the tower blocks that were mainly taken over by New Zealanders, Aussies and South Africans. The tower blocks were marked for destruction, but because we had all moved in, changed the locks etc. We were legal squatters.

===*was the working environment there different from what you were used to*===

Totally different the 1ˢᵗ time I arrived in London, as I didn't have a work permit, all I could get was cash in manual labour, minimal pay.

What kind of working did you do those first couple of months?

I was a labourer most of the time, also got a job once as a window cleaner. It was a recession at the time, so it was difficult getting a job.

===*you also got involved in t-shirt printing. I think we are a bit slow in SA, a lot of those started popping up in the recent past. I believe you worked 12hour shift, how did you find that*===

It was not too bad, there were many good people there and all the banter that goes around helped the time pass.

===*then again, with your own company 12hours is nothing*===

'Working hours' quickly became a thing of the past, especially in the early years. We are a lot more organised now though.

===*Greg, was there no horse racing industry in London? I am just looking at the drastic change of careers*===

Horseracing is a massive industry in the UK. I do not really know how I came to the decision to change careers, just followed my instinct.

===*London became too small for you, so jetted off to San Francisco. Were there better opportunities there*===

My brother was staying there at the time so I went to see him. I also knew that there was a lot of work available in the winter season going in Tahoe. It was not the opportunities that I was interested in there; I just wanted to see more of the world.

===*I am thinking that technology was not so advanced back then, how did you get to hear of these jobs*===

Agencies, knocking on doors, word of mouth, newspapers and friends.

===*jumping from one job to another is something most people did not do a lot then and still do not. First thing that comes to mind is building up a descent retirement fund. Did you ever share this view*===

Not in the early days, but I'm a lot more focused on it now.

===*you got yourself an RV when you went to Tahoe, why an RV this time around? That would be slightly overstepping the boundary of comfort zone a little or should I say fear*===

It was an orange 5.71 V8 Chevy and I still miss it. It had

a bed in the back, with a gas stove. Everything I needed, just part of the adventure.

===*what did you do in Tahoe*===

I met a lady, my brothers had stayed with her before and I asked her if I could rent a room from her. I then got a job at a ski resort for the winter, easy relaxed job.

===*and all this time you were staying in the RV*===

Not at this point, it was mainly in the days when I would be making long journeys or when I stayed in Vegas, I stayed in the van.

===*Greg, clearing snow off people's house for cash would seem like a ridiculous thing to do in SA, but it worked in the US. I am thinking sometimes it's the craziest ideas one needs to come up with*===

It is not an uncommon thing for roofs to cave in from the weight of snow building up; I started working for someone doing this before going on my own.

===*what made you decide to compete with your boss, how was the experience*===

Let me just say it was all done on good terms with him. We were inundated with jobs and he was turning them away, he only had two people working for him. So I just walked the streets knocking on doors where I thought they had too much of a build-up. It was great, nobody ever tried to haggle with me about costs, and it gave me some time to save some dollars to get to LA.

===*knocking door-to-door to get work, that must have been quite a humbling experience. I imagine you were not always welcomed*===

A very humbling experience, the temperatures were way into the minus figures, snowing and knocking on doors. I never had an unwelcome encounter though. Often people would say no and then ask me if I just wanted to come in for a hot chocolate.

===*what happened in summer when the snow was gone*===

In the summer, I got jobs building houses as a carpenter's assistant. I always got great satisfaction from this job as it was very rewarding, building a house from nothing. I also worked as a roofer for a while, very hard labour intensive work. Chopping logs for people's house fires; this was another job that I started on my own when I saw a good opportunity.

===*seems like you were prepared to do any kind of work that you could get your hands on*===

I would not turn down any opportunity; you never know where it is going to lead you.

===*what motivated the move to Vegas*===

I actually wanted a change of scenery and decided to go

to LA, but I could not find any work and apparently, Vegas was thriving at the time with construction, labour intensive jobs. I used the last of my money for petrol to get there. Unfortunately, things did not work out as expected. I ended up eating one hotdog in the week that I was there and no jobs were available. I had to call my brother to send me petrol money to get out of there.

===*how old were you then*===

I was about 20.

===*things did not go well for you there. Looking back with all your experience now, what do you think was the contributing factor*===

I was unprepared. I should have spent more time out there and planned ahead; having no money, Vegas is the last place you want to end up with no money.

===*you decided to go Vegas, you still had the RV*===

I still had my trusty Chevvy.

===*I believe you had to ask your brother for money to come back to LA. How did you feel about this*===

I did not mind asking him for money, he had been through similar situations whilst travelling. I actually used the money to drive back to San Francisco for a few days and then headed back to LA.

===what job did you find there this time around===

I got a job as a driver for an automobile delivery company.

====was there ever a time where you thought that now there's a job I wouldn't ====

No, at the time I could not be fussy.

===before coming back to SA, you decided to make one more turn in London, printing t-shirts one more time, why was that===

I love London; I knew and met a lot more travellers this time round in London. So finding a place to stay was not a problem. Working at the t-shirt place was a good way to save money as they were within walking distance so I did not have to pay travelling costs and they gave us night shifts to earn extra money.

===what job did you do in SA===

Initially, I got a job as a Horse Racing Tipster and racing editor. Whilst doing this I decided to become a jockey's agent again, so was doing both jobs. I then became a Stipendiary Steward for the Jockey Club of Southern Africa.

===seems like you had a passion for horse racing===

I was about 14 or 15 when I first got interested in

racing. It was everything to me.

===*when I chatted with you in 2013, you mentioned there are a lot of business opportunities in London, was that why you decided to move there permanently* ===

I think that was a big part of the reason. I also wanted to have children and for them to have every opportunity in life. The prospects in SA at the time were just not looking great at all.

===*finding work in London wasn't easy this time around*===

Well I was now at the stage in my life where I wanted to get a proper career going, not all the random jobs that I had in the past. I had taught myself programming about 6 months before leaving for London. Unfortunately, I did not have any work experience in this field so I spent a couple of months looking before things fell into place again.

===*what does your job entail these days Greg*===

I inspired the launch of the company in 2001; my role as an Interactive Director is to instigate and oversee projects from a commercial aspect as well as ensuring the best of design & development to exceed client expectations, creating new business, client liaison, managing the day-to-day running of the business, team and projects. I have instigated and manage several shared revenue models with clients of the agency.

===*you founded the company together with your brothers, please take me through the founding stages*===

My brothers and I had gone to a pub for a few drinks. The three of us have always been very entrepreneurial and get on really well. We started discussing how well online games were doing and saw an opportunity to jump in. We had perfect complementary skills. I was the programmer, Rob was the designer and Rowan handled our finances and accounts. At this time and for the first couple of years we worked from our bedrooms before renting property in London.

===*seeing that you grew up together, was it easy to bounce ideas off each other*====

Definitely, we always brainstorm all ideas together.

===*the name Naked Penguin Boy, how did you guys get to that*===

Rob and I were starting an online non-linear comic book. I was to do the programming and Rob was to do the design. The main characters name was Naked Penguin Boy! We then got a call from a friend at Universal Pictures saying that he was in need of a digital agency to urgently take a project and finish over the weekend. So, not knowing anything about the project, we said we can do it. We immediately registered Naked Penguin Boy as a company and the rest is history.

===*how did you guys go about raising capital*===

We did not, we were fortunate enough to have money coming in from the start.

===*most companies need funding at some point. Has the financing been easy to access for Naked Penguin Boy*===

We have never needed funding, got close at times though.

===*what were your thoughts before launching? I guess what I am trying to find out is if you had any doubts*===

I was very confident; I do not think any of us had any real doubts.

===*you guys landed a big job with Universal Pictures, that is quite a big fish you caught. How did you feel about this*===

It was great for us, you could not have asked for a better client to get started with.

===*I believe you gents operated from your houses at the beginning. Why and how did you find this*===

It worked out well in the beginning, but as our client list grew and clients started to want to come and visit us at our offices we had to find an office.

===*the company has gone through recession twice to date. What do you think made it pull through*===

Loyal clients

===*I browsed your website earlier; you guys seem to have built a good reputation in the industry. How did you achieve this*==

It has been through hard work and great customer service.

===*for a newbie entering the industry, what would you say the challenges are*===

There are constant challenges in the industry and I cannot single one out. With everything, you just need to constantly learn and do over and over again until you become an expert.

And the positives

Meeting people, delivering successful campaigns, seeing your project do well on the internet.

===*in Tahoe, you partnered up with your friend and later with your brothers. What is your view on partnership when starting a business*===

It is a chance you take. Partnerships can be very good as long as there's 100% trust between the partners. There are a lot of ups and downs that you have to go through, so have patience.

===*How many people do you employ* ===

Currently there are 10 of us; we used to be 25 prerecession.

===*Greg you have done two jobs twice in your life; t-shirt printing and racing industry. Maybe it was all just a coincidence. What would you say you picked up from these jobs and you still use today*===

It was really in the horse industry that I learnt the most from. It was imperative to be able to confidently work with a team or on your own be the decision-maker. It taught me a lot about communicating with people of all levels.

===*someone coming to London to look for work, what would your advice be*===

Make sure your CV is up to date; make a list of the companies you would like to work for. Get agency contact details and get in touch with them before you arrive.

===*taking out one thing you have learnt in your working life, what would it be*===

Patience & tolerance

===*what do you enjoy the most about your jobs these days*===

If it is a game, we have just developed; I would have kept my daughters up to date with the progress we were making and then just to watch them playing it repeatedly when it goes live. On the other hand, when someone in the office comes in and says that they saw someone on the train playing one of our games.

===*did you ever think for moment in your earlier working life you would be doing work for Universal Pictures*===

Never crossed my mind.

===*Greg, any message you have for upcoming entrepreneurs*===

I do not think it can be stressed enough that you need to have a solid business plan and stick to it. Be determined; think positive!

------------------------END------------------------------

I met Greg back in 2012 in Cape Town and I was intrigued by the fact that he was a South African and had built a successful business in London. When we met any conversation that took place was mostly just jokes we shared. Weeks later, we reconnected on one of the social networks and I soon learnt on the work he did. I learnt about his story and firmly believed that it should feature in this book. The interview was not done live due to the geographical limitations.

When I met Greg the first time, he appeared to be relaxed, down to earth person and not one of many words. One thing I like about Greg's story was the fact that there was no job he would not do, as long as it paid well. I do believe that some of us will run around for ages chasing our on tails before we can find we love doing. Greg story reminded me of how much I fear to cross-oceans looking for opportunities and I am mostly grounded due to my cultural beliefs. I like how he managed to branch out from his boss in Tahoe and taking the opportunity that had represented itself. One of the things that come to mind is how many bridges we burn along the way thinking we will never have to cross them again. Throughout his journey, he could always go back to where he started to find his feet again. He has gone back to the horse racing industry and also went back to the t-shirt printing company to save up some money. When Greg was in Vegas and things did not go well, he did not hesitate to ask for help from his brother

----

WONGAMA BALENI   OF DOC

INTRODUCTION: I am a coffee lover and chances are that if someone told me about a new coffee place in town, I would check it out; this was the case with Department of Coffee. Well first things first , I had never heard of a coffee shop in South Africa's townships, so this made this one an obvious must see. Surprising enough after finding out about the company I soon found out about a gentleman by the name of Wongama, who had quite an interesting story to tell. I had never met Wongama before then and had to make it a point that I got to chat to him

===*Wongama, you mentioned yesterday that you are from the Eastern Cape or your parents are from there. When did you first come to Cape Town and what was your impression of Cape Town as a whole in terms of culture and opportunities for growth*===

I came to Cape Town at a very young age; I think I was 5 years old at the time. My parents had a place here so I came to live here in the township and studied here as well. I did my high school at a school called Qhayiya and I dropped out of high school in Grade 11. I dropped out of school to help my mother, a single mother raised me and I had sisters that I needed to support. My mother was not working at the time and would sometimes send me to the neighbours to go and ask for food. I would pretend as if I am going there, turn around without actually getting there and tell her that they do not have.

===*you mentioned something very interesting there about dropping out of school. We are sometimes forced into decisions however serious the ramifications*===

I wanted to go forward with my studies, but because of the situation at home, I had nothing in mind except for getting a job and supporting my family.

===*how did you feel when you dropped out of school and seeing other kids continue going to school, did you ever feel like you were missing out*===

My mother never had a kid graduating from high school or university and it was my dream to be the first one to do so. After dropping out, I worked for about three different companies and during that time, I wanted to go and study or maybe even try night school. I did a number of short courses and I wanted to have a skill whereby if I go to look for a job, there would be a specific field I could target. While I was out of a job, I went to False Bay College to apply, because a number of my friends would tell me they are completing their studies in 3 years' time. There are three types of jealousy; the first one is the one where you see people are succeeding and you automatically just ignore them; the second one you cannot run from it is nature, when watching people progress and you feel stuck. You want to be in the same position as them or even exchange places. That jealousy thought me a number of things and it can result in you doing something you do not want to do, but you do it because you are jealous of someone else. You can even go to any high school and ask the kids what they want to do next year; a good number will just scratch their heads. In some instances, the person's results may not be good enough for engineering and gets pushed into another course, which was not meant for them. When I visited my friend at this house I would find him doing assignments and he would share his big dreams with me, I was jealous of that, but the question would be what do I do now; I saw him having a successful life. I remember seeing the neighbours had everything from nice couches to cars and I would ask my mother where she went wrong. I would ask her what she wanted to do when she was young and what her mistakes were. I decided that I would change all this, I went to a local college to apply, and they told me I could start next year. At the time I had two options on the table, one was if I got a job I would take it and if I was accepted in college, I would go and study. So when I applied in False Bay College in Khayelitsha, I was not accepted because I failed the entry test. I went to the other campus next to Tokai and they needed a 100% pass in the entry exam and I only got 54%. The person that interviewed me said Wongama next year you are going to study here because you are intelligent; but because I got a job at the Fire Station, I took it. He contacted me the following year and I told him I had to work since my mother was not working. The reason he said I could study there was that I was the only person that said I wanted to do boat building; everyone else wanted to do welding, electrical, etc. When he asked why I wanted to do boat building, I told him that if you are a boat builder, you actually get to do all the other things like welding and electrical.

===*You mentioned two things there, I loved putting things together as a kid, what did you enjoy the most*===

I loved building things with my hands and I remember approaching one guy that was a carpenter working from his garage, I asked if I could work there for free. I wanted to learn how to use his equipment and he said I could work there; eventually he started paying me R50 a day. When I could do the work well he said I could go to Northlink College and I did a six weeks certificate in joinery. On weekends, I was building gates in Camps Bay. When I dropped out of school I had a stepfather who was not keen on me dropping out of school, but I did not want anyone that was going to be the man of the house except for me. My stepfather told me to learn everything around me that I should pick up a piece of paper and read all the time. My English started to improve and then I started to read books as well and understanding things around me better.

===*I read on one of the websites that you were a petrol attendant at one stage, is that true and how long did that part of your career last for*===

I think that lasted for about a year and 6 months. I worked at an Engen garage and made a lot of sales while I was there. I always asked myself if I could make so many sales for another person, why I could not do it for myself; that led to me up setting a braai stall outside the local pubs. I have always been one of those people that put their full effort in a job. My very first job was in a company that made bricks and it was hard work. So at the petrol station I made the mistake of putting the wrong type of fuel in the car and I was told that I will have to pay a lot of money. I decided to quit that job and worked for Total Garage. I think my only problem was that when I worked for a person, I have never had the mind-set that I am an employee, I saw myself as being hired to do my part in the company. I had a problem with the supervisor and I escalated the matter to the manager and still got no help. So eventually, I went to the owner and told him that I happened to have run a little over my tea break while servicing a client and now told that I cannot take my tea break. He never got back to me on the matter so I handed in my resignation letter and that was the last time I worked at a filling station.

===*how did it feel working for a boss, what are the positives and negatives that you picked up*===

You find a negative a boss who just wants you to work for them and it ends there; at some point, you find a boss who wants to build you into a better person. My first boss was a very serious person and wanted to make sure that everyone is strong in his team. He would shout at me, come back 2 days later and invite me for a drink. While we were out, he would tell me that if he did not like me, he would have fired me long time ago; but he loves me and needs me to be there and get the job done.

===*has that helped with the way you deal with your staff members*===

It has helped a lot and I tell them that this is our home,

our company; you are not employed here, you are hired to do your service. If you see that there is an area where we can improve on in terms of doing sales, then put it on the table and let us hear it. I tell them if the company makes money, they also make money as well.

===*that is quite a nice approach you have there. Looking back at your job at the petrol station, you must have dealt with a number of customers in terms of servicing them and so on. Do you think that you apply the same approach and skill to deal with your customers these days*===

I learnt a lot working at the petrol station and I am trying to apply that at my current place of work; I am even trying to get my colleagues to have the same mind-set. When people look at a petrol attendant, they see some who is not educated, but the procedure followed there is good especially for the service business. You deal with customers on a daily basis and you need to have a way of handling customers so that they can come back to you. You have to greet the customer before he or she greets you, you have to show them where to park without any hassle and you have to give them a full service. That is the key point and having done this at the service station, why then can I not apply it in my own business. I also worked as a fire fighter and I had to be part of a team, I am also using that skill when working with my partners as well. There is a movie that I like to watch called "What happens in Vegas ends in Vegas," so what happens at the coffee shop ends at the coffee shop; what happened at the fire station ends at the fire station. You cannot go outside and start talking to people about what your partner is doing, you are going to cause a lot of quarrel. If my partners tell me that he did not like something, it stays here at work and that is it.

===*Well the teamwork was one of my upcoming questions. Was there ever a time when you were working at the service station that you felt like you do not belong there; and can you maybe take me through your thoughts at the time as far as the future was concerned. I think we just sit at our jobs sometimes with no vision of what we want*===

To be honest, I felt as if I did not belong there, like really felt that I do not belong there. I would ask some of the customers what they did for a living because I really wanted to go back to school and study. I was really doing it for a living. I realized that if at some point in your life you feel like you do not belong in a place, you must just stop it immediately. Do not say that you want to move while you are still sitting there.

===*Wongama, the next job you took was firefighting and I am pretty sure that there were some scary times, is there something you could compare the fear to*===

One thing they taught us there was that one should never be a hero. If you take any decision, you have to have a solid plan that goes with it. The job itself was a risk because if we would go on a fire call, there was always the possibility that we will not all come back. If I went inside a house that is on fire, determined that I will bring the people in there out safely is the same to me as putting a million rands in a business planning to get it back.

===*how did you feel when you had to function in a team? Was it easy to adapt or did you ever feel that some of the teams members were just pulling others down*===

On the teamwork, I realised that it could be difficult at times, yes I was more than willing to function as a team. There are people that are totally different and you find them in school also, but we were all told that we brush with the same toothbrush. So ultimately, if I did something stupid for example, it would affect the team as a whole.

===*from what you just mentioned, I am thinking that there are dangers of not working as a team in firefighting, do you think that would apply also in business where you have partners*===

The reason why we were grilled to work as a team is that if something happens to me while we were inside a burning building and I happen to have some beef with my colleagues; they would probably leave me there. They would make sure that we stick together whether we like it or not; so it is the same in a business as well. Imagine if there is paper work or a contract that needs to be signed and you have a partner that wants to go behind your back because you do not see eye to eye.

===*how long did that job last for and what drove you to leave*===

You know people told me that there are no opportunities out there; there are a lot of opportunities out there, but they need people to grab them. I was one of the people that would not stay for even 2 months without a job because I woke up every day and looked for something to do. To get to your question I worked for three companies and I had nothing to show for it. When I worked at the fire station, I was looking for a permanent post and I could not get it. Yes, the money was good, but what if I came to work one day and they told me that they do not need me; what would I do, that was my first question. The second one was about attending a fire call and never making it back. I thought that if I die, I would leave my family with nothing and if I went to study, in addition my certificate would not guarantee anything for them as well. Holding a certificate would hold a better future for me, but not for my siblings. Yes, I was getting good money to put food on the table, but if something happened to me, they would not be able to carry on with what I was doing. So building a business was more motivated by wanting to leave them something they could draw income from. My mother worked for a company and they retrenched her, another one fired her. Time is constantly moving and there is no replacement for time lost.

===I will keep that one in mind. What do think keeps people stuck in their jobs while they are frustrated even if they have a great business idea and will not try to pursue it===

It's fear, pressure from the family side and the way we have been brought up, which is study, look for a job and die. No one tells us to look at the bigger picture, more especially about searching deep inside to see what we really want. No one looks at the footprints behind us and maybe sees that we do not like to walk in a straight line. No one leaves a child behind come back to find that the child has taken apart all the electrical appliances and take note that the child likes to put things together. Sometimes people think that they are keeping their kids from all the bad things. I listen to people chatting about how they took their kids to the park, do the kids even enjoy going to the park? Families do these things because they see other families doing it; what if the kid wants to spend each day practising how to swim and that is what they are good at. I think that is where we lose everything and I think we need to look at ways of transforming the education institutions to be a source of entrepreneurship and not a source of employment. When I talk about this people, tend to think I say kids should not go to school and that is not the case. We need to engage a more practical and enhance the skills kids show instead of killing them. There are schools that have engineering as a course in high school and when those kids get to tertiary they immediately fit in, this is not the case with some of the township and rural schools. When those kids get to tertiary, they face the dilemma of not even knowing what to study, that is what I mean when I say education is poor in a lot of areas. I started going around the community and getting kids to come and work at the coffee shop to get exposure of the business world. I tell them they should go study and when they get their qualification, they should consider going into business; soon they will see other doors opening. We are sometimes pushed into decisions because of roll models or we want to compete. There is a book called "Two roads to cross," when you see someone driving a nice car and that person is a billionaire, we would choose to follow that even if it is not what we want. A typical example is how kids see a gangster driving a nice car and is lucky enough to stay in a nice area; they will simply follow that path. You get two kinds of people, those who want a job and those who just want to work, it is better to have the latter. To get back to your question you have employees and then you have entrepreneurs; the two live on completely separate worlds. An employee will get a job, get wages and have fun. An entrepreneur will first be creative, get the job done, make a profit and have fun.

===*so how did you overcome the fear of leaving your job and were the people closest to you supportive of that*===

That is a difficult part and as you mentioned earlier that there are people who want to leave their jobs and venture into business, but they cannot overcome the fear. You know my mother had this old bed and an old cupboard so when I was working in the beginning; it was just about putting food on the table. When I eventually got the job at the fire station I was getting a good salary and I started buying my mother nice furniture and made her house look nice. My mother was happy and she knew that on the 27th of each month, we would eat out or I would bring some take away because I got paid. I would buy my sister's kids shoes and everyone got comfortable with the idea of me having a decent income. I told them that I am planning to quit my job and they were not happy, we went on fighting about his. I told my mother that I have a child and if I die now, they will continue living the same way they have been living. I told her there is a chance that I could end this if I did what I wanted.

===*a good percentage of people in their twenties are more concerned about partying and going out, what do you think motivated you guys to drift away from that life*===

They always say if you want to be a billionaire, you must start acting like a billionaire now. They also say that you must start being responsible, but when we started our company, I still went out partying. I realized that on Mondays I would struggled to make it to work and I had a friend that would tell me about how he arranged a sick certificate to give to his boss. Now if I took his advice, to whom would I give the sick note? I would be robbing myself. I realized that I had to change the company I kept and find people who were like me. This goes back to my point earlier about the two different worlds an employee and an entrepreneur live in. I will say though that if I had not done all those wrong things at the beginning, I would not have learnt anything. That is why I say to people that it is good to fail and if you have never failed then you must know that there is a problem. When you fail, you experience something different and you fix the problem. One of the reasons people are scared of failing because they are afraid of what people will say. Imagine throwing a tennis ball on the ground when it bounces, it goes higher. So it depends, when you fail, are you prepared to bounce higher. Look at how you fail and find out how you failed instead of being worried about what other people think.

===*you are in partnership with two other gents, how did you all meet*===

We met around the township. My friendship with Vuyile has been one where we helped each other and gave each other good advice. We have always respected each other and got things done. Vusi grew up around the same area as me so we became friends. We started an organisation that was doing meditation and there was a gentleman that was teaching us from Cape Town; he would come out here once a week. When we started, we were young, jobless and there were about 30 of us.

The number dropped down to five because people wanted to see the results now. It is the same with business when people see an opportunity; they want it to make money now. I told them that we should keep on doing the meditation something will come up eventually. There was a guy that was doing a documentary at a place called Mzolis and all I kept on saying there when I was interviewed was that I wanted to have my own business, I wanted to be a businessman. The gentleman came looking for me at the fire station 2 years later and asked if I still remember the interview. He opened his laptop and kept on playing the video as I repeated the words "I want to be a businessman"; he then asked me if I still want to be a businessman. I told him that I still want to be a businessman and he wanted to find out what type of a business do I want to open; so I said I will get back to him. Vuyile and I sat together and started to look for things to do. I met a guy called Peter in town and he told me that he has the money we needed for funding, but we need to do things correctly and be able to pay him back. He did not say this in a polite way and since we started the business I would sit and think of the tone of voice he used, it really scared me. We started by running a carwash and a Laundromat because of the pressure we were getting from our families. We walked around with this bag full of paperwork, just paperwork and no income. The 27th of the month would come and I was not getting a salary as I used. I would have some doubts sometimes and think about going back to the fire station. So we approached these guys and told them we do not want them to borrow us money because we want to buy food at home, but we have an idea. We asked them for an old washing machine and asked that they print flyers for us. The plan was to open a Laundromat at my mother's place and it operated very well. One of the gents had a golf club and when we visited them, we asked if we could do a carwash there because we saw that there are a lot of cars. They allowed us that and we did well there. Eventually we did some research about coffee and we decided to go ahead with it so we closed all the other things and focused on the coffee business.

===*were the other businesses doing well when you closed them*===

They were not unique. They needed a lot of time from us make more money. The main reason is that we wanted to do something different and unique; the investors also did not want us to do a Laundromat, as it was not unique.

===*can you take me through the thought process when you were generating an idea, the branding and picking a location to operate from*===

Firstly, we wanted to do a business in the township as there are too many businesses in the CBD, this also had to be something that attracted tourists as well. As we were braining storming the idea of coffee popped up and to this very day we still question ourselves who's idea was it? When I first heard the coffee idea, I thought one would have a kettle, instant coffee and that would be it. One of my partners had experience in the coffee industry and he took us out to the CBD and showed us the coffee he was referring to. As we did the research, we started seeing more opportunities. We did a micro MBA course where they taught us about running a business, from a business plan, stocktaking and money management. The people that invested in the business are also business people and they would invite us to events and launches. We would get there; see people dressed in fancy suits and feel like we did not belong there.

===*Wongama funding is normally a stumbling block for most people wanting to start a business. How did you guys find this*===

In the beginning, getting funding was not easy, it is still very difficult. People apply for funding from banks and government, what has worked for us is asking individual people. To be able to get funding from individuals you have to do a practical business plan, not necessarily write it down. We could have asked someone to write it down for us, but we would not be able to answer the questions if the bank asked about something on the business plan. We did a practical business plan, stood outside and counted the number of people that were passing here; we could tell the funders that there are more than 5000 people passing here every day. It is the same thing as when you apply for a job and they need someone who has 5year's of experience, they have done their practical and also know what they are talking about.

===*in your view what are the benefits of a partnership in a business and how has the experience been for you*===

It is not easy to be in a partnership because at the end of the day, we are all humans and we have different views at times. It is part of the journey and you need to come up with ways to make the partnership work. As I said earlier "what happens in Vegas stays in Vegas," we have adopted that into our business. I think most partnerships that do not work out because of people keeping all the baggage with them. It is similar with relationships as well, if you keep on hanging on to all the baggage and letting outsiders in, there will be problems.

===*in my chat with you earlier you mentioned that once one enters a business, they start seeing a whole lot of other opportunities that one cannot see from the outside. Can you share what you saw once you started*===

When you standing outside, you will not really see what is going on. When we started our coffee company we thought we would be standing outside the shop selling coffee, we never thought we would be supplying big companies like PSG and doing events. Someone will say that they want to be a policeman when one day, but once they are inside, they start seeing other opportunities all the way to being the police commissioner of the country. I was in Pretoria a couple of weeks ago and I was sitting at a restaurant where their coffee did not taste good; that was an opportunity right there to ask if I can supply them.

===*you get individuals who stand firm that your idea will not work, how did you guys overcome that*===

When we did our research, 95% of the people said the idea of a coffee shop in the township is not going to work out. We had to overcome such by doing and make it happen. When you still have an idea, funders will not see it as something they can put money in. When you execute your idea well and make it happen, funders come running to you wanting to see your financials.

===*you have also managed to attract tourists to your coffee shop, how was the feeling when you saw that happen*===

It was exciting times and when you are an entrepreneur people will have lot of doubts when it comes to your ideas. That is where you need to be executing your plan and if it does not work, you come up with another one. If you are selling t-shirts and they are not doing well, look for another way to sell the t-shirts instead of giving up. We were located near the railway station so we approached the company that runs the trains and approached the tourism companies to give people a tour. Even when it's hot outside, white people still drink coffee and that is when the black locals also saw they can also drink coffee when it's hot.

===*the media coverage you have received, has it helped to bring out people your direction and getting the marketing going as well*===

The media helped us a lot in terms of getting the word out there. After we were operating for 2months, we asked one of the local radio stations to give us a slot for our marketing purposes and they told us the fee was R16 000. We went back to our funders and told them about this and they told us no ways. We stood outside the coffee shop saw that we created something unique as long as we worked hard. After the first media company approached us, things just exploded and I do not remember a time where we had to pay for coverage. I do advise other entrepreneurs that they must come up with something unique so that they do not pay for media coverage; your business must have a story to tell. You need to be changing in a sense that when someone that was here last year comes back again, then that person must find something new. When one gent came here the first time he saw me selling coffee, he came back again and I was selling coffee beans and t-shirts, when he came back the third time I was training young people about how to run a business. The next time he comes around we would have opened a new store, so all the time I am changing. I will contact the media again once the new store is open and they will do the marketing for us.

===*you guys are kind of giving back now in terms of training, what else do you do*===

We are giving back to the community in such a way that we are donating to the local crèches. Then we also train younger guys the skill of running a business, but also try to impart the skill of doing things in a more practical way. I want to change the perception of people only working for bosses; I want to transform the entrepreneurial spirit into young kids. One of the kids said to me the other day that we cannot all be entrepreneurs, but half of us have a good chance.

===*sounds like you are doing quite a lot of giving back. What do you see as a key to keeping the doors of a business open*===

You have to be able to get the job done to the best of your ability; you must be able to take risks even when the business is already operating. You have to be able to make sacrifices and run a business for at least a year and a half without any income. There are people that pass here and we know them, they will sometimes ask for money because they can see it is busy. Now you have to able to overcome such as these people do not know where the money came from and how hard it actually is. I am not good with computers, but there is what they call a recycle bin. When you are starting a business you need to put all your friends and family in that recycle bin, if the business does well you can always come back to pick them up. Do not try to impress them by handing out money when the business is still new.

===*would you say that the community has changed the way they view you guys now since started running the business.*===

I think we have inspired a lot of the younger guys when they see the outcome. We sometime get university students who ask us for assistance on their assignments; it is not only university students, it is also high school learners. Even the jealousy I felt when some of my friends were completing their diplomas is no longer there because some of them will tell me that they are still looking for a job.

===*where do you think you guys are heading in the near future, you have mentioned already that you are planning to open another coffee shop*===

I do not want to be a billionaire, but we would all like to have money one day. I want to see us with more stores, creating more jobs and assisting the community as much as we can.

===*if you were to start another business what would it be*===

My dream has always been going into property, but at a large scale. I would like to own an estate one day, a community.

===*what is the one thing you have learnt from when you left school to now*===

One of the things I have learnt which I also do not believe at times is that I have managed to do something that seemed impossible. Today I am running my own business and I face the difficulties. I never thought that I would be on TV and newspapers one day; I always thought you have to be an actor to make it on TV. So with hard work anything is possible in life. If you want something to be possible, you have to give it your utmost best.

===*any words of advice to upcoming entrepreneurs and guys who feel like they stuck in the corner in their careers*===

Start thinking outside the box, this does not mean you have to leave your job. You can easily look for opportunities within you place of work.

------------------------***END***------------------------

As soon as I checked out Department of Coffee (DoC), I discovered that three gents in total founded it. This got very interesting later as I tried to get hold of Wongama to schedule an interview with him. What I have found was that it is not easy picking up the phone and explaining to a person what it is that I do and on many occasions, I am met with a number of questions that I find difficult to answer. When I contacted Wongama and requested to schedule an interview with, he said I could chat to any of the founders; I cannot just single him out. This was almost impossible for me to do as it took me about 4 hours to prepare for the interview, meaning I would have to spend about 12 hours. Later as I was preparing for the interview, I picked up something about Wongama, in one of his previous jobs he was a fire-fighter and that immediately alerted me about the kind of bond he will have with those he works with. There is a saying amongst fire-fighters *"It's all about the man next to you, that's it, that's all there"*. Equipped with this knowledge, I knew I had to change my approach and approach them as a team. I took the morning off to go and meet them at the coffee shop and speak to each one of them explaining what I was trying to do. I soon felt like interviewing all of them as they all had a remarkable story to tell. They were all very welcoming and Vuyile (one of the partners) took me through the stages of getting the coffee to the customer starting right from the ground. He shared the importance of all three stages for example how the guys doing the roasting must do it well, how the barrister must make sure that they burn the milk at the right temperatures. As I was being educated about this I noticed the third partner Vusumzi was busy educating a group of young people in the other corner. I later found out that DoC takes young people from the community and educates them about running a business. I decided to grab a cup of coffee and a muffin; I was told that for every muffin they sell, they donate a certain percentage of the money to the local pre-schools. By the time I left to prepare for the interview I had a complete understand of the culture at DoC and it was quite something to write home about. Growing up, I watched a number of school kids from the early grades right to the last one dropping out of school. In the early ages, most of them had no guardians that would play the "guardian" role in their lives and others dropped out due to financial situations at home. I have watched a number throwing their lives away and they are now begging on street corners. I have also watched a handful of them rise up, taking charge and beating the odds; Wongama's story reminded me of those kids. This reminded me of the famous quote by Bill Gates, "If you are born poor it's not your mistake, but if you die poor it's your mistake"; to a greater part, Wongama's story was a promising reflection of that.

Wongama had to make a number of difficult choices in his life and many of which could have had serious repercussions had he for once lost his focus. One of the things that drives him, he mentions a number of times is the need to provide for his family. Wherever he felt uncomfortable, doing what he felt he could not be doing, he found the means or a way to get out of that situation. More often than not, we tend to settle for things we should not be settling for because we are scared of wondering off into untouched territory. I have come across a few people who worked as temporary employees at major companies and one gent retired as a temporary worker with no benefits after more than 20 years of service. Wongama had kind of found the life he wanted to some degree which was helping out his mother and being able to buy things for her things, but this was not enough. It takes a lot of gut and taking of a rigid personal inventory to reach that point. I personally had to say goodbye to a decent job that provided an average person's needs, I relate a lot to the decision he had to make. I also find that people like Wongama are able to move on when the circumstances are not favorable for one to stay around. When he moved from one job to another, he portrays the same attitude when he moved from running a Laundromat, carwash to the coffee shop. What I learn from this is that one should not marry a situation that is not conducive. They ran the Laundromat for some time before seeing that there is no room for growth and they eventually gave it up and moved on. This also goes deeper in our lives and a simply analogy I like using is one about being chased by a dog. We are told that it safer to just lie down instead of running, more often that this is not the case, we would rather run for our lives knowing well we cannot outrun a dog.

I do like the part where he also talks about the

company one keeps; sure thing we cannot dump all our friends, but keep the ones that are contributing to your course even closer. Around this part, he also mentions his dilemma with a sick certificate from the doctor and he realizes that in a way he would be robbing himself. Again, this goes back to the point of a rigid inventory and seeing when a situation is not working. I remember opening my first start-up and for some reason saw, it fit that the money be deposited into my personal bank account. It was great knowing I had money coming in at the end of each shift, but the problem came when I had to pay staff and buy new stock at the end of the month. This meant that I had to now draw from my own personal account and pay for the shortfall. I could have opted to continue that way, but in truth, I would have closed up shop eventually.

"If you know the enemy and know yourself, you need not fear the result of a hundred battles." The trio could have chosen to open the coffee shop in the CBD and competed with the Goliath's, but they knew that the competition would be fierce. What has also put them on the front papers of the magazines was the fact that they were operating from the township. They chose an area, a niche' they knew very well and dominated it. Before them, there was no coffee shop business in the Cape Town townships.

CHAPTER FIVE

Here Be Dragons

"Our weaknesses are always evident, both to ourselves
and others. But our strengths are hidden until we
choose to reveal them--and that is when we are truly
tested. When all that we have within is exposed, and we
may no longer blame our inadequacies for our failure,
but must instead depend upon our strengths to succeed
... that is when the measure of a man is taken, my boy."
— James A. Owen

SIZWE NZIMA OF **IYEZA EXPRESS**

INTRODUCTION: I was driving from Cape Town
to visit my folks in the rural parts of the Eastern Cape
Province. For some reason about 230km from Cape
Town I turned on the radio, which is not something I
do often; you see I am the type of person that organises
the audio CDs to play in the car long before my trip
and will just listen to them the whole way through. As I
drove up the mountain pass in the De Doorns area I
listened to a discussion on radio about this young

gentleman that started a company called Iyeza Express and had managed to dominate his niche. The first impression I got was that this is way too easy and very simple and about 200km later I was forcing my brain to think. I could not start the next Iyeza Express, but the story itself motivated me to find something new, exciting and never been done before. This led to me coming up with First Idea. After listening briefly to Sizwe Nzima's story, I was motivated and I felt that if his story could motivate me the way it did, then surely it could do the same for someone out there as well.

===*Sizwe over the past 2 weeks I have been coming to Khayelitsha mostly for work. Do not get me wrong I used to come here to party and all of a sudden, I am seeing this vast world of entrepreneurship taking place. Do you think it is ignorance that makes people unaware of this or maybe short sighted of what is really taking place within Khayelitsha*===

In my view, the perception that people have when it comes to Khayelitsha and other regular township is very dull. Not to say you are dull, but even the media portrays townships as a dull place that is unlikely to succeed because of all the social problems, crime and poverty. So it is a very dull place for people to be able to say that your next billionaire is coming out of Khayelitsha in a shack. Your next Patrick Motsepe, there he is sitting on a shack with the family of eight in one shack. People do not expect those types of things to happen in a township. There are a lot things happening in Khayelitsha, what I can say is that there has been a lot of movement when it comes to entrepreneurship. People are starting to realize and come up with ways of improving their ways through business. The problem I have which I have raised with the government at conferences is the fact that it is called informal because it is not compliant; we are running businesses here what is informal about a fair trade taking place? I give you a piece of meat and you give me my money, everybody is happy, what is informal about that? I think they call it informal because it does not comply and it goes back to what you were saying earlier about people being raised to comply. If you do not comply with the South African Revenue Service, you will be seen as a big threat. Yes, regulations are good, if there were no regulations this country will be in a mess. Instead of going on about companies that are not compliant and closing opportunities, why can they not just show the companies how to become compliant according to the law? You cannot just say it is informal because there is a formal trade happening whether the contract is on paper or it is verbal. Even in court a verbal contract is still binding, yes a written contract is more concrete. Even though there are many businesses in Khayelitsha, people still view them as informal because of certain things that do not meet their requirements. Those things still close a lot of doors for small businesses in Khayelitsha to grow because of these compliant issues.

A typical construction company goes for a tender and they do not win the tender if they do not have the required documents regardless if they have more than enough qualifications, but how easy is it to get those documents. So those are the things people are pointing at, the bad things. There are many informal businesses, there is lot of crime, there are lot poor socio-economic conditions, but they fail to highlight that there is a lot of movement when it comes to entrepreneurship. I promise you even though it is a copycat movement, but there are great ideas coming out like Lufefe Nomjana, Sizwe Nzima and Melilizwe Gqobo with Hubspace. Typical example spinach bread comes out of Khayelitsha, a simple logistic company like the one I run; I do not remember hearing of a logistic company based in Khayelitsha. DHL, FEDEX, UPS are all big American companies and it shows that there is a lot of potential. To answer your question there is a lot of potential in Khayelitsha, it is just that people are not tapping the right spaces to find it. If you go to a party clearly, what you will see is people partying, but if you dig deeper and you go to places where entrepreneurship is happening, you are going to see entrepreneurs at work. There are people who have PHDs that are from Khayelitsha so if you are looking for them you have to go to where they are. So people are missing out on a lot of potential because of the overall reputation of Khayelitsha.

===*I totally get what you just said there and you also touched a bit on my second question, we are seeing the winds of change through the youth. In your view do you think that starting the business in Khayelitsha also gives you that advantage that when you start you are a unique business, the media and funders coming running out*===

Well it does help and even where I am now I have a partnership with Metropolitan Health for about 2 years. Somewhere, somehow, I was on the media and then the Forbes listing happened that is when they started recognising Sizwe. They followed Sizwe because of the great idea and the great impact he was making throughout the community. Through that, they decided to partner up with me to grow the business, so yes the media has benefitted my business in terms of being in Khayelitsha. As you said earlier that you discover one cool idea and then later you discover there is a string of ideas connected to the first one. This is quite personal information, some of the things I am working on. I discovered that through the delivery model of medication I have a better understanding of Khayelitsha geographically, much better than Google. There are areas where Google will not have the right street name or not have it all, but I promise you that you just give us your address and we will find you. That is how core Iyeza Express is and we have managed to say through that we can capitalise on that skill because that is a skill we have. You cannot buy local knowledge and we employ people from within the area. The person that lives in Makhaza, delivers in Makhaza, he knows Makhaza in and out. There are places that Google Map cannot get to and cannot give you a street name, my driver will get you there. We have a special team; we have a special company. We have managed to say that we are going to be building a logistics systems in townships. What you currently have is a massive economic growth-taking place in the townships; people are starting to move into townships. People are getting comfortable with going online and buying things online and what does that mean; more logistics. Even with the DHLs, FEDEX, UTI, they still consider townships because of the crime, but guess what, we have never been mugged and have never been robbed. I am now working with a company called Laser Logistics, so Laser has asked how they can be part of Iyeza Express. Iyeza would then become the last-mile extension so if they have any deliveries in Khayelitsha, they would apply the last-mile extension. For them to navigate this area, it costs them a lot because of the fuel costs, risk and the number of return parcels or lost. What I came to understand is that through the delivery model of medication, I will develop a model that is utilised and franchised through every township. Through that, I can then say I own township logistics and if you want to get anything into the township, the only person you will speak to is Sizwe. The media has worked for me getting people from outside the township to help and the second one is the opportunity with Laser Logistics. For them to actually come out and talk to Sizwe was something big. UTI is also a company that is planning to do home deliveries and they can only do that through some local logistics company when it comes to the townships. I would be lying if I said that there is a company out there that understands township logistics better than Iyeza Express does. That is an opportunity on its own for the company.

===*It sounds like a positive move for the company. If you look at the future of the township itself, where do you think it is heading in terms of entrepreneurship*===

As I said, there is currently a lot of movement in terms of entrepreneurship locally. For us African Black people, it was not a common thing, growing up our fathers worked in the city and the mothers were housewives. For most of the years for us, it has been about going to school, getting a good education and going to work. People are slowly starting to understand the rewards of entrepreneurship as compared to working for someone else. People did not see the opportunities because they were focused on one routine, which was the common routine that history embedded on us. It has been all about going to school, getting a good job, get a big house and by the way you are still working for this person; you get your pension and after that life is done. People are getting to understand that we do not have to follow that routine.

Our minds are waking up through education and obviously through creative thinking skills. I see the community is slowly being attracted to entrepreneurship; yes, it is still not the trend, but in a couple of years' time, it will be the next big thing. Everybody now wants to be able to say, I built something or I built that business. They are starting to see the opportunities and they are slowly starting to understand that life does not have to be a straight line. Life allows us to be creative, but history has embedded into us that life should be this one path where you work for a boss until you retire.

===*Sizwe, I am slowly getting the idea that the best age to start a business is below 40, this is just taken from the small sample of people I have interviewed. Richard Branson of Virgin Group seems to think 30years is kind of the cut of limit. What is your view on this and why do you think this is the case*===

There are many things happening around that specific age and I think it is easier because the brain is still fresh. Once you have a family, kids and a wife, the only thing you have your eyes on is the bonus at the end of the year. I think a number of things would come to mind like how will you support your wife, kids and so on. All your responsibilities rely on that particular salary and having to leave that job becomes very difficult. From my side I think that is why people over the age of 30 will find it difficult because they have families. When I started my business I was 20years old, still supported by my parents. My brain was still fresh, but it also gave me that room to move.

===*What do you think could make more of the younger people participate in the change that is taking place? More often than not you will find that people from other countries come here and participate in the economic cycle*===

Just to clearly highlight the age factor again, it gives me room to experiment, but that is also very difficult. This is also attributed to the history with our parents and I am also getting this from my parents why am I not going to school, why am I not getting a job, is this thing going to work. Those are questions we get and you are even asked why you are wasting your money. When it started even my grandparents asked why would I want to start my own business, but as time went on and they saw that the media is slowly projecting it as a good idea. All of a sudden, they say it is a good idea, but because the monetary value has not come in the way I would like it to come, I have not been able to buy the things I would like to buy. They still do not trust it though because there is no instant cash flow. I think one of the reasons is that in the African black family you have to start by supporting your family and then build your own life. Those things are still expected of me, but because I am still at a young age, it gives me room to experiment. At a younger age, the brain is fresh, you have ideas, and you see things differently compared to a 40year old. At 20 or even now, I am not scared to try out new things. That is why you find that the best people to be managers are the older people and the best people to come up with ideas are the ones who are still young because their brains are still very much creative. You get the experienced brain that actually knows how to focus on systems and the bad thing about the young brain is that it lacks focus. I also struggle with focusing also because I get a lot of ideas and ideas flow, you then need experience. Being 40 years old helps because you understand how things need to be done, but it has its limitations in terms of your creative thinking. To answer the next question of people coming from outside the country and we are not participating, we as South Africans are not pioneers; we lack that. There are only a few pioneers in the country and this I mean people who have the gut to go and start something new. This is not about copying what is there; it is about the gut to start something new. A typical example I always use is Spaza Shops, I am doing research on Spaza Shops because I am looking at ways of how I can change the model. I am looking at how can I change the model and set up a franchise of Spaza Shops. So I am currently looking at a lot of things and a lot of ideas, but this one interested me because Spaza Shops are a South African thing; how do you get beaten at your own game. Yes this happens sometimes, but one should be able to bounce back easily. Somalis and the Bangladeshis came here, took over the Spaza Shops and they used only four key elements to achieve this. They had better distribution; better stock, better systems and they were pioneers. The reason why we are not pioneers is that we are scared of starting something new. Pioneers are not afraid to stand alone in the community, but we like to fit-in with the normal structure. If you stand out, you seem a bit odd and the rewards of being odd is that you become the role model within that particular sector. As much as we want to stand out, we are scared of diverting from the normal route in terms of starting your own company as opposed to going to school; which is also not a bad thing following the normal routine. In South Africa, we talk about "Ubuntu" (humanity), but Ubuntu can be taken to another level. One of the analysis I look at is how Muslims operate their businesses, now that is what you call true Ubuntu. If you go into their shop to buy something, they will not tell you they do not have the item you want while the next-door shop has it. They will rather go around the back to the next shop, buy it there and come back to sell it to you. Alternatively, they will tell you to go to the shop next door and will tell you that they work together; I have called the person and he is waiting for you. What does this tell you, they do not want money going out within their own sphere; they will rather go out of their way to make sure that you get the product particularly somewhere else. On a business level that is on another level of Ubuntu because they make sure that within their sphere they help each other to grow. With us, it is different, yes, competition is good, but we have the kind of competition that can even kill our businesses. It does not become healthy a competition because you find that there are two carwashes opposite each other and the one is talking badly about the neighbour; rather than just competing on simple services. You can just highlight the benefits of your service and let the client buy on the benefits of the service you give rather than badmouthing each other. People are seeing these gaps and are utilising them. Like you mentioned earlier we are scared of being pioneers and there is only a few pioneers in Khayelitsha your Lufefe's, the Sizwe's and the Vuyo Rani's. These are the people that will say this is odd, but I prefer being odd. In a couple of years' time, these people are seen as leaders in their communities. The one country that still portrays the most pioneers is America. There is something called the American Dream, where people dream of being billionaires. People in the US are naturally pioneers, they are not afraid to stand out and be market leaders. In our country, people are very cautious and we are reluctant to become pioneers.

===*to a certain extent, I would think that starting a business early in life would mean no more partying and going out. All of a sudden, you have to grow up quickly and take on the responsibility of hiring people. How was the experience since you started quite young*===

It is very difficult and even more difficult now. As a

young person, you always want to go out and enjoy life, but I think for me, it is still difficult. I am the youngest out of all the people I work with, but I still have to take on the responsibility of managing them, showing them how things are properly done. When things are not done properly I have to take action, those are the things that I am not accustomed to. As I learn through the business, I become more and more prepared. I just studied an entrepreneur course and as I slowly grow the business, my brain is becoming more open to certain things. What drives me the most, there a person when I was at school that said, "As an entrepreneur the first 10years I will live a life that no one would ever want to live, but in the next 20years I will live a life everyone is dreaming of living. What he meant was that, what I am doing now might be difficult, it might not make me feel good compared to going out with my friends, but in the next 20years, they will want the life that I will be living. The vision of living a better life still drives me, I still get tempted to go out, but sometimes you find that I have cash flow problems. My life becomes boring compared to other people even when I look at it; it is boring compared to what I used to know in high school. It is not easy, but I believe that it is bound to pay off. I think I will live the life most people will be dreaming of and yet not acting on it. That is the thing we do not understand as people, what we do now has an effect on tomorrow. The fact that I am sitting here now actually has an effect on tomorrow; in economics, they call it opportunity costs. What is the opportunity cost of me being in the office drafting down a strategy plan as compared to me taking 5hours to go to a party? The opportunity cost of drafting a strategy is the fact that after that strategy has been implemented there is a financial gain to it. The opportunity cost of being at a party is the fact that after the party there is cash lost, yes there are emotions attached to it. So what are the opportunity costs there and how important is it for me to party now. I look at the bigger picture which is when I have a family, how do I want my family to live? It is all about the future as opposed to the present and that is why the present does not really affect me the most. In the future, I clearly do not want my children to grow up the way I grew up. I clearly want to live in a nice place one-day even though my business will be based in Khayelitsha; I want to experience life beyond just living in a shack. For me if I could get a chance to buy a house in Camp's Bay, I would buy it tomorrow.

===you managed to earn a spot on Forbes, how did that make you feel in terms of where your business was going and what did this mean for you personally===

It has two sides to it at first, I was shocked and I thought are these guys sure it's Forbes. The people I would see on Forbes are the Patrick Motsepe's, the Johan Ruperts, I mean all the big guys; I honestly could not believe it. For me personally that made me feel good because I believe I am pioneer and I have set history. When I read the local newspaper, it said "History being made, first Khayelitsha business to make it on Forbes." As a person who likes leading, I felt like I have set the benchmark for Khayelitsha and obviously the Lufefe's came on board. People like the Luvuyo Rani's who operate a very successful internet café came to me and said he is proud of me; his business was much bigger than mine was. I still had less than a 100 patients and he said I have made history, as I am the first person to be listed on Forbes from Khayelitsha. That was a big achievement for me and to some people it might seem useless because there is no financial gain that came with it, but for me setting trends is a big thing. On a business level, this made me understand that the potential my business has is far bigger than what I had in mind that is what opened up my mind. The rating was for "30 entrepreneurs under the age of 30 in Africa," not Cape Town, not South Africa, but Africa and that told me that this business has the potential to grow. It is bigger than Sizwe and way bigger than what I thought it would be. That is when I thought I am on the right track and it gave me more confidence to say that Iyeza Express is bound to be successful; I just needed to follow the right track and do things the right way in terms of managing the business. The idea itself is a successful idea. They say that most good ideas do not become good businesses, but I understood that I have a great idea and that I needed to work on it to make it a good business.

Through understanding that idea and understanding the potential of it, I then understood that if I could turn it into a good business, it could reach high standards. On the other side to explain things further is that it gave me a lot of pressure because suddenly, now you are on Forbes, let us see what you can do. So every day when I experience bad things I sit and think what are the people going to say. Now that you can lead, people expect you now to show them what you can do. It has a good impact, but it also affects me on a level of pressure, so I have this pressure on my shoulders that I should succeed. Yes, some people are waiting for it to fail and are waiting to say there goes Iyeza down the drain. Some people will say that he still has potential because the Richard Branson's have showed us before that they have failed and made their way up again. Failure is common and I find that most entrepreneurs who have made it, they have failed before. It is a common thing to fail as an entrepreneur when you do not do things the right way, but other people view it as the end of the world. So yes, the Forbes listing attracted a lot of media and also gave me the pressure that I needed to prove myself.

===*I like what you mentioned about failure there, I recently did an article for my small blog on failure and the title was "At the face of failure – The lesson missed." It was about seeing failure as nothing but a lesson. Sizwe you mentioned that you might not be where you want to be in the first 10years, what do you think will drive you the most in that 10years. You have also touched on*

cash flow problems and not being able to support your family like
you want, what drives you to continue===

What drives me is the dream and desire to go beyond normal expectations. People were not expecting the next Forbes listing will be from Khayelitsha living in a shack at the back of his grandparent's house. I like going beyond expectations, what people think or expect of you is not entirely what should be. People might think I am from Khayelitsha, but for me, I do not see myself living in Khayelitsha for the rest of my life in a shack. I want to prove to people that despite where you are, it does not determine where you are going. Secondly, for me, it is about giving my family a better life and yes, they might not be getting that now. It is all about the dream of living a better life and the desire to defeat expectations.

===just to go back little, were you born in Cape Town===

I was born in Cape Town, grew up with my grandparents and everything happened in Khayelitsha

===what would you say you enjoyed the most when you were
still young===

I have enjoyed helping people, I am a very active person, and I have a lot of energy. I have enjoyed helping around the community. There was a gent that I would assist when I was growing up; he sold chips and cool drink. I was involved in the awareness program as

youth going around the schools addressing the HIV
awareness programs. What I do find interesting is that
there was entrepreneurship embedded in me when I
was growing up. My mom sold a lot of ice cream when
I was growing up so I used to go and get stock for her
at the wholesale; I knew what was going on in terms of
getting stock and selling it. This later came in handy
when I was at the Raymond Ackerman Academy as I
enjoyed participating in entrepreneurial activities
especially those that had to do with helping out in the
community. I still remember that arrangements were
made for us to attend a camp and I did not have
enough money to go to the camp. I also did not have
enough money for my taxi fare to get there, but
fortunately through the academy, I got help in a couple
of things. I still had other problems and one day I
remember having R6.00, thinking I am going to buy
something nice. I went to the Lavazza coffee shop and
saw these nice big muffins and I thought they will be
going for R4.00, I was told they are going for R12. So I
walked up to the vending machine and the only thing I
could buy was a packet of chips going for R5.00. From
there I told myself that this is outrageous and a couple
of weeks later I bought muffins in town. I bought them
for R10.00 a pack of three and bought Doritos in a box
after having saved up some money. We attended classes
with a number of MBA students and some were
working for big corporate companies. I would stand at
the courtyard and I used to sell the Doritos for R3.00

and the muffins for R5.00; I would sell all my stock every day. Then one day the lady who was an administrator asked me where I got the right to sell these things there because my stock was just flying. Friends of mine were already helping me, so entrepreneurship was there. Unfortunately, I was told that I could not just sell there, so I had to stop.

===*Sizwe how far did the schooling go and did you have any idea what career path you would follow after finishing*===

I finished matric and my dream was to become a lawyer, so I always had an interest in law; I mean who would not like those big gowns, big briefcases and suits. My friend, Lwando and I have always wanted to study law and he is still in law today. I did however add an extra subject while in school which was Business Studies. Somehow, I have always liked the way things run in business. When I pursued my legal career, I got so bored; to be honest I got so bored with the reading, the atmosphere and everything else. For me it seemed like I would go down this one path, every day going to school reading the same books, writing the same long essays, you are marked and it starts all over again. I felt like we were studying the same thing every day, the origin of law, the Roman-Dutch law. It got to a point where I asked myself that if I understand law, what is next. It was always going to be the same law line even if it was different court of law. That is when I tapped into my second career option, which I have always looked at as well, and that is when I tapped in the Raymond Ackerman Academy, which is a 6months entrepreneur course and as far as that goes, that is the only schooling I have. I am now pursuing my degree in Supply Chain and Logistics. I fell in love with logistics and the movement of goods and came to understand that there is money to be made in logistics.

===*In terms of work experience, do you have any other experience besides working for yourself*===

That is one of the things my aunt always motivates me on, I have worked as a waiter, but I was still at school and paid cash. I have also volunteered at a golf club. One of the things my aunt always says is that I am lucky as I have never had a payslip and from the way things are going, I am never going to have one. I know how a payslip looks like, but I have never had one in my name. I do not remember having a payslip saying "Sizwe Nzima working for company ABC."

===*Sizwe what were you expecting to gain from the Raymond Academy Program when you went there and how was the outcome*===

When I went there I was clueless, but I just wanted to get into school and get into business. At that time, I was not accepted at the University of Cape Town for the business course. At first, I thought I will get into the academy, get experience and then I would go and work. When I got there, things totally turned out different and I could say that they tapped into the underlying entrepreneur. That is what they managed to do and I thank them for tapping the entrepreneur within me. I was maybe afraid to show it, but within 6 months, they managed to tap into it to see my true potential. I am very surprised to be where I am and to be honest I have never pictured myself to be where I am, even when I was at the Raymond Academy. Back then, I did not believe much and when I came out of the Raymond Academy, I really believed what they tried to instill in me, that I was born to be an entrepreneur. They preached that to us the whole time because they could see certain skills and certain attributes. I think there are certain attributes one shows to be an entrepreneur. The thing about be me being a pioneer, I heard it from them when we did certain activities while camping. They told me I am not afraid to start new things and I would rather bend the law to start new things, I would see the repercussions later. I do have a potential to become an entrepreneur.

===*what I am getting from most interviews is that passion plays a huge role. What does passion mean to you when running a business*===

Passion is the fundamental; it is the most important thing because without passion, you have nothing driving you. For me without passion I would have quit a long time ago. A couple of months or a year after I started and the money did not come in, I would have stopped. Passion keeps on reminding me about the bigger vision, the bigger goal I want to achieve. If you do not have the passion, you lose interest and there is a high chance you are going to quit. Every day I am not rich when I go to bed and I am not rich when I wake up again, but there is a thing that tells me that I want to be rich and I want to make it. Every day I go to bed with a small amount of cash flow, the next day I wake up with more problems even bigger than my cash flow and yet, something tells me I will make it that is passion. Passion is what drives me every day because I sleep today not knowing what is going to happen tomorrow. Then suddenly things are going well, the next day I sleep very dull and wake up the next day I am motivated. It is an emotional rollercoaster, but passion keeps me motivated all the time. It should drive you forever even if the business is as big as Coca-Cola, you can easily quit without passion. If you have passion, you continue to run it every day regardless if there is money or not.

===*I think I should hear this directly from you, what is it that you guys do is and in what year did you start operating in* ===

We started operating in 2013. What we do is quite simple, we collect chronic medication from public hospitals and we deliver them to the patient's doorstep. Our core aim is to minimise the process of having to get your medication, which is very long when it comes to public facilities. We have seen that process as truly unnecessary where someone could be sitting at home and get their packets delivered to them. Instead of them using transport and standing in queues, we do it for them. As time went on, I would say that we provide logistics in township areas. We are now working at having a proper logistics company, but also having a medical courier distribution company. Our advantage is being able to locate the township maze and through that, we can be able to deliver other products.

===*I do not know how true this is, but I read somewhere that you started out by helping your grandmother get her medication*===

The idea came from me being in that particular situation. Where there is a problem, there is an opportunity and I saw it; I did not believe it at first, but I saw it. I was the one collecting medication for my grandparents and at the Raymond Academy; I used to miss class sometimes because I had that responsibility. At first, I read an article at school about how hospitals could not cope with the influx of chronic patients. While I was sitting there I thought to myself I know this problem, but is there another way of doing this. That is where the pioneer came in; is there a way to change this because we are now changing a process that was designed by the government. So as I sat there I thought that there is another way of changing this and that is when the idea of a bicycle courier model came in. It was all through a problem that I was in and because I wanted to get out of the problem that led me to actually want to change the whole process. I was sitting on a gold mine, but I did not know it back then.

===*mostly you will find that people have brilliant ideas, but are scared to carry them out due to a number of things. What advice would you give to those people*===

No one knows and no one can really predict 100% what the future holds, we all take chances. Even the person who has a job, they do not know if that job will still be there tomorrow. Why do you think when you have a job you are safe, why do you think you are safe at anything? I can die tomorrow, I can build a business tomorrow, and I can fail tomorrow so the trying to be safe does not always work out. It is my own theory, but we are never safe. If you are scared to start your own business because you are scared of failing, losing, who knows you might wake up in the morning with a business as big as Coca-Cola. Because we do not know the future, all we need to do is to believe in ourselves that is the only thing we can do. We just need to believe that tomorrow is going to be better, you can never be sure, but it allows you to go forward in life. I really see life as a gamble; we plan today for something we do not know. Why should I be scared of starting a business not knowing what is going to happen? Rather go in, start a business and you fail, there is a lesson to be learnt.

===*you mentioned that you were the youngest in the company, was it easy for you to give instructions to people older than you*===

It was not easy and it is still not easy especially with us African black people, there is a whole lot of respect element attached to someone that is older than you are. When you give instructions to someone older than you it becomes a bit awkward even to the person you are giving the instruction to. I have managed to tell the employees that there is nothing personal here, if you do something wrong, I am going to tell you. If we are going to grow this business, we need to work together because you might find that there are certain things I do not know that are happening on the ground. I do not think it is about giving instructions but more of coordinating and making sure that things happen the right way. It is not about me making myself feel better, but coordinating and making sure things run smoothly. They might tell me that the way I said we should do things is not working and then show me an alternative. That allows them to see it not as an instruction, but see it as advice on how to do things better.

===*Can you recall the most challenging time when you started out and perhaps just delve a little in how you pulled yourself through*===

The most challenging time was when I was being chased out of the hospital. It is an interesting story because I first came with two patient cards, which belonged to my grandparents. After sometime I came with a couple of cards again and they asked to whom the cards belonged to, I told them my grandparents, my mom's and the woman that lived next door. The next time around I came with 10 cards; they took me to the facility manager's office and said I was selling drugs. They said I was taking people's medication and selling it. I came clean and told them that I am pursuing the opportunity of collecting medication for these people. I used to be chased out of the clinic and when I arrived there, I could hear the staff saying here is that child that sells other peoples' medication. Sometimes the clients would come and complain because certain things were not included; it was the clinic's problem. The staff at the clinic would tell my clients that the problem was that they let me take the medication instead of collecting it themselves. This dented the reputation, but I told myself that although I am not a pharmacist, I am going to try and make sure I understand what is happening in that industry. Today I understand a number of things like scheduled medication and know what medication is stronger than others are. That is the basic information I have, and I had to equip myself with this knowledge. That was the most difficult moment because I thought if I do not find a way to work with the government, then there is no business. I simply overcame by speaking to the facility manager, brought in some stakeholders from the Raymond

Academy, and that holds quite a good name. Things started getting easy there because they managed to contact some people in the province who are in the department of health. So I pulled strings and I still remember Mr. Ackerman asking Francois who does he know at department of health, so Francois led me straight to the provincial office. I met a gent there Cloete, who manages all the hospitals in the province and he guided me to the right direction. That is how powerful the name of Raymond Ackerman is and you have to use those types of names when you have them. In the end, it really helped.

===*I know sometimes at the beginning you struggle with staff members because they do not see the bigger picture. At times, there is no money to pay them, how did you get them to see the bigger picture*===

Well I have always shared the vision with them and yes, I have had staff that left because of money; I have had people that stayed. I always tell the guys that are here that where we are now is not important, what is important is where we are going and want to be. Life does not end in a day and what people say to you today should not affect you. I share the bigger picture and what stands in benefit for them, imagine starting out at a big company, it takes years to get to the top. It much easier to work your way up in new a company, anyone that comes in after you, will have to be trained by you. That means you are growing as a person as compared to working for a for a big company getting paid better and still work 10 – 20 years as a receptionist. If you work here as the company grows, you will grow and technically speaking you become part of the company. I try to tell them that they must not think of it as just putting money into the shareholder's pockets, but they also get a chance to grow in their career as well.

===*what has worked better for you, was it word of mouth or the media*===

It has always been the word of mouth. The media has worked in terms of attracting funds, sponsorship, opportunities and carrying the name up in terms of building connections. Word of mouth and going to the clinics to get customers is the best, people want to see you face to face. Old people are not trained to use some of the technology; they prefer seeing the person face to face. I remember someone was asking why do I have my face on the banner and I told them that people want to know who they are dealing with. Even with my drivers, the clients know who brings them medicine; there is a sense of trust, a sense of attachment because they can see you.

===*would you say that the community views you differently now or do they still think of Sizwe as that young volunteer at schools*===

It has changed a lot because people are now starting to look up to me as a big business person even though I am still very small. They look up to me in a sense of they have seen what I can do, they have seen the potential and they also want to follow in the footsteps as far as business is concerned. I think it has changed from just being a normal person to being a role model in the community.

===*so looking at other businesses, what would you start today if you were to open another business*===

It would be something in the pharmaceutical industry.

===*so what would you say your typical working day is like*===

I get up at 06:00 and my room is right next to my office so I do not have travelling time. So I wake look at the information, what do I need to deal with today and look at my plans for meetings. At 08:00, I am at the clinic because the clinic opens at 08:30. I take the medication and sort it out; I am back at the office around 10:00. We split the medication according to the geographical areas, the staff delivers them and I go to my meetings. I come back to look at the overview of how things are going and from there we catch up. From there I either go to church or follow up on my appointments for tomorrow. So yes, my life is quite boring.

===*Sizwe you have had quite an interesting journey, however short. What would be the one thing you could say you learnt===*

Well through everything, the one lesson that I have leant is perseverance. I never imagined any of these things in front of me when I started at the Raymond Academy; I never thought I would have an office. I never thought I would be associated with big companies such as Metropolitan; it did not come into my mind that I would be associated with Forbes, but through perseverance, all these things came through. I persevere even now; I still believe that there is more rewards to come.

===words of wisdom for upcoming entrepreneurs===

Well just go and do it, stop procrastinating as it is one of the things that kill us. Get rid of the "I am going to save money up and do it when I have money" or "I need to build connections first"....then you will find another problem. One of my lectures told me that a business will always have problems. We all think that Coca-Cola is this big fantastic problem free business, go into Coca-Cola you will find that there is huge problems. If you are going to stop and identify problems, you are never going to start. When Coca-Cola started, they had problems and they still have problems today. Start what you want to do now and deal with the problems as they come.

-------------------------END-------------------------

I set out to contact Sizwe to arrange an interview with him and from the first time we spoke on the phone, he was rushing to take a taxi to attend a workshop. I managed to briefly introduce myself to him before realising that I have caught him at a bad time; he did ask that I drop him a message for the appointment. My second attempt I caught him while he was about to enter a meeting with the suppliers and this time around he asked that I call him around 16:00 in the afternoon. I soon realized that he is a busy man and not easy to get hold of. We managed to set up an interview for the following Monday. I drove to this office a bit wary if I will be able to get hold of him seeing that he was quite busy as mentioned. Upon arrival, I learnt that he was still at the hospital and his phone was on voicemail. I was met by two company employees as I entered doing admin work and the other was busy uploading new clients data. In front of him was a pile of application forms of new clients and he informs that the company currently delivers medication to 8000 clients. I tried finding as much information from him as I could although he was willing to answer some of the questions, at some he balked. I could sense the feeling that he did not want to give away much detail without permission and I explained the reason for my visit. As I was sitting one of the company riders came in and told me that Sizwe is at the hospital and he could take me through to him. I went with the gent, and he told me how busy things were and for the first time ever they had to work on a Saturday. He was also excited about the battery-powered bicycles the company just got, saying he could now make up to 25 deliveries a day.

I caught a glimpse of Sizwe's face on local websites and so it was easy for me to spot him amongst the hospital crowd. We met and he apologised that he had lost his business cell phone during the rush of that morning; well he said he was frustrated and I just saw someone who was very relaxed. He stressed a bit about how all his contacts were on that phone and one of his major suppliers must have been trying to get hold of him. I later pick this up from the interview when he mentions that problems will always be there; I for one would stress about losing my personal cell phone for a while before finding my calm again. The employee that I had driven with collected a box of medication and he was to take this back to the office. Sizwe opted to cycle back to the office and told the employee to drive back with me. It was around then that I got my second impression of the relationship between Sizwe and his employees; let us be honest most employers would have told the employee to cycle back while they drove in the car. This later comes in light during the interview when he says **"we have a special team, we have a special company."** From personally experience, there are number of things I did not like when I was employed, to be undermined, to be controlled and not feeling like I belonged. Although he is the youngest, he has to rise to the occasion when it is necessary.

The employee I drove with took me through the office and showed me the main company operations, the boardroom and storage room. I was taken to Sizwe's office where the interview would take place and this question crossed my mind a number of times "at the age of 23 what was I doing?" The interview with Sizwe commences and he apologises about the delay. By now I have learnt a number of things about Sizwe and the one important thing I could relate to is doing one thing day in day out, he refers to it during the interview as "routine". What we are constantly taught is to concentrate on one thing at a time and surely this works for some, but you get a different group of people who would complete three tasks in one day rather than one. If for some reason you force this group of people to complete only one task, they will never get anything done. This later comes up again as Sizwe shares his future plans about building a township logistics company, his research into Spaza Shops and trying to come up with a model of improving it. Again, there the norm is to concentrate on one thing until you have done it properly before moving on to the next. He reveals this again at his attempt at law school where he got bored of the routine, not because he did want to go to school, but he simply got bored. What comes across is the level of confidence he carries, he has a vision and believes that it will happen, not if it happens. Just from the start, the examples of companies he uses are world known companies the likes of DHL, Coca-Cola and

FedEx. He is not afraid of mentioning them and also how Iyeza Express is even bigger than he is. He has an approach with regard to problems that left me with a different view of facing the problems I encounter in everyday living; **where there is a problem, there is an opportunity**. I remember in my early school days that some of the kids would only be able to attend school 3 or 4 days a week, other days they were burdened with family responsibilities. Sizwe shares something similar to this when he says he would sometimes miss school to help collect his grandparent's medication from the local hospital. I am sure most people can relate to the feeling he had when he only had R6.00 with him and could not afford to buy muffins, this problem represented an opportunity for him. He did not just accept that he could not afford the muffins he did something about it. This skill comes up again when he was faced with the problem of the hospital not allowing him to collect the medicine for the patients. People who have attempted start-ups will know that at the beginning mostly anything that can go wrong, will go wrong.

I was also made aware of the pressure he has to deal with from cash flows, pressure of living up to the Forbes listing and most importantly pressure from his family. With all this in front of him, Sizwe does not say that this was enough to stop him. One of the most important things I have learnt during the interview was remaining positive. Throughout the interview, I do not get any sense of doubt from Sizwe, everything he does; he does with passion and the drive to succeed. He does not say "IF" I make it, he knows he will. He managed to start his business within his community where he knew what the challenges were and as a result, he has a better view than the bigger logistics company.

Sizwe has volunteered in his younger days and that is something we do not want to do, we want the quick money and we want it yesterday already. What has been interesting enough is that he volunteered in the health sector and how he has helped his grandparents to get medication. Towards the end, he mentions that he would choose a career as a pharmacist and the signs have been there for some time in his life. We know what career path we want to follow from a young age and sometimes it is right in front of you the whole time, Sizwe is yet another great example of that.

LUFEFE   NOMJANA   OF   ESPINACA INNOVATION

INTRODUCTION: I am in Khayelitsha, Cape Town chatting to the founder of Espinaca Innovations and hopefully I am pronouncing it properly or that might just cost me the interview. I first read about Lufefe on a friend's Facebook status. I guess that is what we are missing in life, make things simple and just stay focused. And at a distance I have kind of managed to watch for news on his company. Subsequent to that, his name has been popping up on a number of websites and people talking about his company.

===*Lufefe the first time I read about you I think was on a News24 website and I imagine you have had a number of companies coming to check out what are you doing here; how has that experience been*===

It has been in fact a great experience because it is an exposure on its own. On the other hand, it has been the word out there for us and what is important as an entrepreneur is that you want to be known, to be acknowledged by the world. The companies, the media and everything that has been happening around us has showed us that we really are innovative. If we did the same things as you mentioned earlier that we complicate things by doing them the way society wants us to. If now we come up with a way of doing things differently, we become unique and then the world would follow us. In as much as it is very difficult to bring change because it actually entails a number of things that are considered unusual.

===*if you look at how people view you now around the neighborhood, friends and family, would you say now they view you as someone they can look up to or do they still see you as that young boy they have always known*===

It has been as struggle starting this business and someone can easily judge you on your past or who you were then. It is still unbelievable to some people, but I have changed a number of people through my character and the ways I have developed myself through innovation as well as coming up with something that is impacting the community. So it has been a journey that has been impacting people in my community as well, I have young people that have been watching the way we do things. Also having interviews like these with people who want to change and it has been an experience of giving back as well.

===*one of the interesting things about you is the fact that at the age of 23years, I was at the prime of my partying life and I guess nothing much has changed out there around that age group. What motivated you to decide that now is the time to grow up*===

There was something at the back of my mind that motivated me especially when I looked at the problems and the challenges of my community. It was a wakeup call as to I needed to change the society and that was the big and crazy thing at the back of my mind. I listened to it because it kept on persisting that I needed to change the community and I knew I had to change myself before changing the community. I had to educate myself about things and the personal development started there, but ultimately I was motivated by the problems of my community.

===*based on what I read on one of the websites, I believe you also had to change your eating lifestyle and become a vegetarian.*

And on that I had lunch with my daughter on Monday and thought I should maybe try some vegetarian food it was quite a challenge finishing the dish. What made you change your eating lifestyle===

For me it just happened automatically, it was a natural thing after I realized that I had to change. The second part was more of wanting to volunteer before I could actually change. Change for me was to impact and from impacting I knew a solution would come. I went to a community garden called Abalimi Bezekhaya and that is where I volunteered for a period of six months. As I worked there as a volunteer, I then developed the love of vegetables and spinach itself; at the time I was living with my fiancée. I thought if every day I am getting vegetables with no income, living in someone's backyard in a shack and I am getting spinach every day, then I am already a vegetarian. I had been a vegetarian for six months already and I am not eating meat because I could not afford it, so it automatically happened; to this very day, I am still a vegetarian because of that garden. Coming out of that garden has taught me the skill of permaculture, growing vegetables organically and secondly the idea of incorporating spinach in daily-consumed products derived from the garden. The love, the passion for spinach came from having to volunteer in the community garden.

===so you are telling me this had nothing to do with Popeye Spinach, not even a small chance===

It has to do with him because I grew up watching those cartoons and when I was looking at this spinach every day, I just knew that there is something about spinach. It has never been promoted the way it was promoted back in 1945 and beyond through Popeye Spinach cartoons. So let me be the Popeye of Khayelitsha, let me carry on with the legacy of spinach and ever since then it has not been promoted the way we are promoting it here.

===*been doing a bit of reading of lately and one of the stories I found fascinating was the one about Walt Disney and how he used to draw pictures and sell them to his neighbours. Eventually, when he came back from the army/Red Cross, he started drawing and that is how Mickey Mouse and the rest of the characters came about. So I guess it's always something in our background*===

Yes definitely, that correct.

===*Lufefe what does your company do and please do forgive me if I am not pronouncing properly, Espinaca and perhaps delve a bit on why that name*===

Yes, it is Espinaca and I chose Spanish because I was looking for an international name. I was looking for a name that was appealing to everyone because the vision was bigger than the shack I lived in, the environment and Khayelitsha. I was just looking for a name that would appeal in the world and I went searching on Google for a spinach foreign name. To be honest "umfino" would be very limiting; that is a Xhosa name for spinach. I decided to set-up a company that would not only benefit my community, but the world at large in terms of expansion, franchise and branches in the near future. I had nothing in the pocket, just that vision and a bit of intellectual capital. I chose Spanish because it was easy to pronounce than Espinianzo, whereas Espinaca is more appealing and you know that it is spinach.

===Lufefe more often than not we tend to do things the other way around by starting big and fancy and by the time we realize we should have started at a small scale, it's too late. You managed to keep your overhead and operate from home, yet managed to bring out tourists to your place. Other people would want to start in Sea Point or the Sandtons of the world===

I needed to start somewhere and as I mentioned earlier the plan was to impact my community in as much as the broader vision was to diffuse the same concept to other areas. I had no choice, but to start where I was and the way I started was very innovative on its own. Apart from incorporating spinach, what has been very important was the way I started the business and it was very innovate. I guess if I were in town, you would not be sitting with me and having this interview, but because where it is today, it matters to the story. It is funny how I started because I only had the bunch of spinach, R40 in my pocket and the intellectual capital, which I normally say, is the capital that is sufficient for anyone to start a business with no capital in terms of currency. That intellectual capital is what led me to the neighbour next-door because as we did not have an oven, we had a two burner stove which was not good enough for the vision. The shack in its own was not conducive to the idea and the dream we had, I was aware of everything and I knew I needed a kitchen that is hygienic so I could not use the shack for this particular concept. We started from the neighbour's oven and the neighbour was actually very happy to assist in giving the spare capacity of the oven when they were not using it. I started baking from 03:00am up until 06:00am because at 06:00am that is when they would start to prepare for work and get the kids ready for school. I would work 3hours, knead my dough from my shack and make sure the fermentation process is done in my house. I would be whispering during the night baking only four loaves of bread and for me that was important. It is not that I did not go to other areas and look for ways of assistance like funding, resources; I spent my fair time there and nothing came. Everyone would say it is a good idea, but they do not think that spinach bread or the green bread is what is going to sell. Some would say I needed to go and do my research; that was the response I was getting when I went outside Khayelitsha. I would try to mingle with people and ask them for assistance and no one was there. What is important, as I had mentioned we started humbly from this community and that made us reach out to those communities that rejected us when we were just an idea.

=== *I am going from one company to the next asking people for the chance to interview them; it has been a humbling experience for me going around asking people for something. Did you find it easy to approach your neighbour*===

It was very easy; I was driven by the passion in me. Before I approached my neighbour, I sat down and pulled on all my thinking caps and there was no other way I could start this business. The only way this would work would be to approach someone who has what I do not have. It was easy in a sense that I only needed a spare capacity; I did not say that I was going to use the whole kitchen as my business, just a spare capacity. I had a dream to make sure that I baked a product that would change the industry and change the world. It was not a friendly thing, I pitched for that and I knew I would knock on their door and if the answer was no, then I would continue knocking down the street. Fortunately, she agreed and allowed me to use the oven, which is where we piloted everything; selling three loaves, a day and the other loaf would be for sampling and tasting. I was making a loss and every day I would go to my family and ask for a plate of food for me and my wife. It was all about the passion more than the profits. I did that for about 4 – 6 months, they saw the persistence and the commitment; they said we can see that you are here every day at 03:00am so we kind of trust you now. They said they would give me the keys so that whenever they are at work, I could make use of the kitchen. I was so happy because this meant that I could now bake between 16 – 24 mini loaves of bread a day; I was using her pans, her everything. From there we were ready to upscale.

===*as men we often think we should be doing the hard labour outside, I for one cannot even bake, but will try something out one day. When did you start baking*===

It was a process of me having to research; it was part of my intellectual capital. That is why I believe that I am learning anyway and there is the internet. I did not know anything about baking; I knew how to bake using a bakpot (three-legged pot used for cooking on open fire) in the rural areas. I did not know how to come up with a professional loaf so I went online to a website called Breaducation; I searched for "how to bake the world's best bread" and that is how I came up across the platform. It is a platform that teaches you how to actually bake an ordinary basic loaf, but in a good quality. I learnt the process of fermentation, which is more the raising of the dough, the temperatures, the kneading, measurements and the baking itself. I got everything online and I was applying it as I was baking from the neighbour. In about a month or two, I was the best baker in the town and I taught my wife how to bake the same bread; I imparted the very same skill I got from the Breaducation platform. What was so innovate was that I could take that and modify it into what I want. The process is basic and fundamental, what I infused there was different; so I would take out what is not relevant to my belief and my passion. I took out the white sugar and used a bit of brown sugar, I took away the salt so the bread was sodium free, white flower was replaced by brown and I used olive oil. That was my formulation; my method of doing it and then I thought let me now incorporate spinach and you do not what to know how I did that (both laughing). It was a trial and error, experimenting with different ways to bring the spinach in and the bread did not taste good. The bread was not delicious and people were looking for something they could taste than something that is healthy with no taste. It was a hustle trying to come up with delicious bread, but healthy; I wanted to change the perception people had of healthy food being boring.

===*I am interested in finding out about the first loaf that you ever baked, how did it come out* ===

It came out well brother I do not want to lie because I was applying the knowledge from Breaducation. The process was good and everything was just fine; I was very happy and it felt as if I had all the millions in the world. I felt like I had everything I needed having that bread come out of the oven and I still have some pictures of it. When I went to sell the bread, I remember being paralyzed for 15-20minuets because I saw Albany (one of the biggest bakeries in the country) offloading about, 10-20 crates at some spazashop and I had only four loaves. I remember standing frozen looking at my four loaves; I looked at the way in which I am selling this bread and I compared it with them. It was fascinating and there was something in my head that said it is a David and Goliath story, we will get there.

===*Was there a bit of fear in that instant*===

No, no, no, no. No fear at all, I was like, we will get there and that will be us. You will be amazed how we are selling in stores today. We are beating the competition; we came in number at 10 in Van Gate Mall in the top 50 sales and Albany came just behind us. That is due to the military strategy we use which is more of selling than putting bread on the shelves. Today we are selling about 25 loaves of bread an hour and in most cases, we sell whatever we distribute to the stores every day. We are using a military strategy knowing that we are small.

===*I guess that is one of the things that should keep one their feet. I am thinking now as I was preparing for the interview I kind of compared baking and starting a business. As you mentioned you play around with the ingredients until you get what you want. Do you think the two go hand in hand*===

Having the skill of baking is another hustle on its own, remember you are not employing anyone here you do it yourself. After that, you have to go and sell, that is the entrepreneur. The business starts when you sell, that is the transaction. The two combined require skill and discipline whereby you can bake and make sure you can sell what you get. Baking is very different, like cooking, most people can cook, but cooking to sell is different. For me baking and selling were the same because as I was baking, I was burning on the other side to sell. There was a burning need for me to sell this bread because I believed that it was something that needed to be diffused to everyone. As I was baking, I had the burning desire to sell the bread not because of profits, but someone had to get this bread. I knew that someone would pay for the bread, it was small like a mini sized loaf and I was charging R10 for that. Everyone would say it is nice and different bread, but I would also pop in with maximum passion. I would come in your house whether you are doing laundry or you are in the bathroom I would say keep on doing what you are doing, I will just do my talking. So before I sold I would be juggling four things because I was baking, doing health education, sampling and marketing. It was not about the selling of bread, but the education about the healthy eating and the healthy lifestyle, which I had just adapted from working in the garden. I would pop in saying "Imagine bread made from vegetables", what you are eating is not made out of vegetables; you are going to work now and do not have time to prepare yourself a vegetable meal. This bread consists of all the vegetables you need and some ingredients that will actually benefit your health. I would tell them about the nutritious value which I learnt from the internet and while I was working in the garden I developed the health consciousness. There were workshops and people would come and tell us about the broader spectrum of nutrition. I became a nutritionist by default and I was imparting the information to people whom I was selling to.

===*when you started, was it a matter deciding that you will start with only bread and later add other items at a later stage*===

The bread was the flagship. The company name is Espinaca Innovations, which simply means Spinach Innovations. I knew that I would make spinach tea, spinach juices, spinach smoothie, pizza bases and in everything I would incorporate spinach. We had to start with one product that is highly consumed so that on a business point of view we can make money and have cash flows for us to build another range, which are muffins. Muffins are not consumed as bread is and after muffins, we made spinach rusk; we also cater to tourist at events so whenever they come we cater a spinach range of products.

===*you went looking for funding on thundafund.com and had a good business plan on that. I recently came across someone who paid R25000 for a business plan, what do you think is best hiring someone to do it or doing it yourself*===

A business plan is your vision, your dream; it is what you want and should not even be more than 10 pages if your business is not a 10-page kind of a business. What I can say is that I did my business plan myself and I never approached any consulting firm for that. Even if I hired them, I would have to sit with them and explain my vision and where I would like to take the business to. I would have to tell them how many loaves do I need to sell to breakeven or to pay my expenses, those are all things they will get from me. I see it as an unnecessary cost to hire someone to record my thinking; I would rather record my own thinking. A business plan was a guide for me, the business and for me to operate within the business itself. There is a business plan for funders, which is more of projections, yes, projections will help me, but they are for funders as soon as they infuse cash. Thundafund was the innovativeness of using what you have because I have developed a humble way of using what is around me. I have spent so much time looking for funding, knocking at doors for financial assistance and no one was there. I decided that enough is enough, let me use what I have and I went online; for me the internet is one of those currencies that need to be used and a free platform you can use to get whatever you want to get. I needed bicycles because I had people delivering muffins on foot and by the time they have to deliver them, the muffins would be cold. We did not have a car, let alone afford one. I sat down again; I normally force my mind to think innovatively at any situation in a business. Every time I find a challenging situation, I force my mind to think so the idea was to go to the internet once again. I searched for innovative ways of funding and then came across crowd funding and Thundafund was that platform. I read about it trying to get more information what this is, what I needed to do. All that it said was that I needed to run a campaign and then the world would fund me. People around the world, people who I have never met up to this very day, funded those bicycles. Everyone was giving us money after looking at the pictures and the moves. We said wanted five bicycles, branding equipment and t-shirts for us to get by. Every day we would post pictures of what we have done, pictures of when we went to the garden, delivering bread at the crèche. People were so fascinated and inspired to put more, we exceeded the limit because it was R5000 and we got R11500. It is mainly because of how we ran it and in about a month or two, we got the bicycles. Yes, the plan was to have the people run around delivering bread so I wanted a concept that would grab the attention of the world once again. I wanted something that would show the people who funded us that what they contributed towards, is actually working and bigger than just what they thought. So we had another campaign and named it green bread on bikes and we would drop the bread at your door step. Symbolical the bicycle symbolises the healthy life style, as you know the bicycle is eco-friendly and its carbon footprint is what we need for green purposes. The bread symbolised the healthy eating so we were beating two birds with one stone and everything was just conceptualised mainly because of the platform we got from the internet. Fair enough today, we still have some bicycles and we still do bicycle deliveries.

===*the very first sale you made, I am thinking you got your bread tasting good, how did you convince the very first customer to buy it*===

It was through going from door to door it was neighbourhood selling. I would bake from 03:00am to 06:00 and at 06:30; I would be at someone's door. People answered by asking what is it now; I would respond by saying "The Green Bread" that was my greeting. I would have a loaf with me diced into pieces so that people could taste the bread. The bread was wrapped with a plastic wrap, I would give them a sample and while they were busy tasting, I would be talking and explaining what is it that they are eating. That whole time I would be explaining the ingredients and the importance of eating healthy.

===*has your approach changed now when you go to the bigger clients*===

It is still the same approach nothing has changed. Yes, you have your normal bread, but this is the future of breads.

=== *tastes like the future* ==

No, you have only tasted the muffins; you will get to taste the bread later.

===*I believe you also went to do a course at Pick 'n Pay or so*===

That was way after I had started the business. It was a customized training and I told them I do not want to learn they you wanted to teach me, I have a different concept. They said it is fine and asked what is it that I wanted to learn? I told them I wanted to do a basic nutrition course within 6 weeks on a part time basis. They taught me that and now I am a nutritionist by virtue of attending that and as well as by virtue of being a volunteer at a community garden. I am also a baker which I learnt from Breducation and cooking from Pick 'n Pay. I told them that I want to cook using vegetables even with the recipe we sat down and developed a number of recipes. It has been a journey like that.

===*growing up as a kid what would you say you enjoyed the most. I know for a fact I loved putting things together, not to say I was good at it though*===

I wanted to have a life that is different from other people; I wanted to be a farmer. People would laugh at me and make fun of that. We would stand up in class and some would say they wanted to join the police, be a soldier and I would say a farmer. Really, I had a vision of being of farmer because at home, the other families would have plenty of land and we would have to go there to ask for maize. It made me want to be a farmer so that I could provide for my family the things we would always have to ask for. I was also the child that was out there, I was an average child, but I knew that there was something different and special about me. I knew that there was something wrong about the way I was being evaluated in class. I looked at people who were seen as the clever people in class and I would think to myself these people are not clever, but yes the results they are getting are quite good results; but I do not think that this person is clever than me although I was getting zero per cent.

===*interesting you should say that because First Idea is about showing people that. Interesting you should also say you wanted to be a farmer; there is a farmer I chatted to recently. He said that once in your life you will need a doctor, a lawyer and a teacher, but you will need a farmer every day of your life. At some point Lufefe, I am sure you had to hire staff members and I am assuming that there were times you could not really afford to pay them. Did you have any kind of arrangement with them*===

I knew from the beginning I could not afford to employ. I would hire someone and would tell them that I do not have a job for them; I have an opportunity for them to put bread on the table. The only way we can do that is if you cooperate with me and how do you cooperate with me is that I will give you the product and you will have to be a businessperson and take the product to people. I will show you who are those people, but I need you to take the products to those people and sell it. Any business is made out of sales and I saw commission as what would work for me. At that point, we did not have cash flows to pay such expenses. My wife was baking while I was also baking and selling. I would be assisting them with the selling and then assisting my wife with the baking, so we did not pay for a baker. The people doing the selling paid themselves through commission and it was successful.

===*your longest serving employee, how many years of service do they have*===

We have two founding employees and others left us because they did not see the bigger picture that we have always been preaching. We kept on preaching that we will be there; we will be there in just a short period of time. When the preaching time came, a person would get wary of waiting for the bigger thing to come. It has been a journey like that and we only have two people that have been with us ever since we started. Today they are sitting with salaries and working comfortable.

===*something I forgot earlier, how many years have you been operating for now*===

Since 2011 when I started experimenting by myself and

in 2012, we started operating so it has been 4years.

===*Lufefe if you look at the R40 story, we tend to think we need thousands to start a business. What would your advice be in that regard*===

Raymond Ackerman always says that need 90% guts and 10% capital, which is true. As for me, I would say you need 95% guts and 5%, capital because that R40 was maybe 0.00001% of the capital I needed. I had no oven, no ingredients; I only had R40 and an oven from a neighbour and baking pans. All of that was too expensive for me, but I was utilising those resources without me having any 20%, 40% capital. It was just leveraging and using what is there. They call it bootstrapping where you join a number of things and then once you have joined all those you look for ways to accelerate things. So ultimately, the acceleration is that 5% or 10% capital.

===*Trick question Lufefe, I give you R40 to start a company today, what would you start*===

Now that is a tricky question. I would go and buy bunches of spinach because I have good relationship with the women at the garden I volunteered at. I would buy three bunches for R10 because that is the partnership and deal I have with them. I would buy about twelve bunches and that is about 24 loaves so I can do something with that.

===*who was your first big client and how did it feel*===

I remember after working at the neighbour's oven the demand was growing exceedingly and I needed to find ways where I could capacitate the business. Capacitation of business was to look for a giant, an existing place where I could bake from, or a facility I could use. I had been in business for 6 months and had zero profits to show. The business was just operating from passion, debts from the family and contributions from the family. I would call a brother from Johannesburg and ask if he can bail me out with R100 and he would deposit the money at Shoprite stores. After 6months the demand was more than the 16 loaves I could bake from the neighbour's oven. I went to a local retail store, Spar in Harare and did the same thing I did when I approached the neighbour to get that oven. I got there and told the people, "here I am the Spinach King of Khayelitsha, I am known here and I have a market share." The reason I am coming to you is that I have a problem and they asked what the problem was. I told them that my product is in demand everywhere and I cannot produce more. I am looking at ways in which I can maybe even sell it to you; I am running around because I do not have a place I can sell from. I am baking from home and I am running around selling to everyone, it is consuming time, energy and the time I am using to go around is supposed to be the time I am using to produce more. They said you sound very entrepreneurial young man, and what is it that I

have. I had my bread right there and looking back it
was a joke; it was a small loaf wrapped in a clear plastic
wrap. I then asked them to taste it; it is the spinach
bread, the future of breads. Firstly, they said that they
do not think I am ready to approach them, as I did not
have a proper package; secondly, this is Khayelitsha, do
you think this will sell. I remember telling them that is
why I approached them; it was because of the demand,
I even showed them pictures. They told me to go and
get funding and then come back to them to talk again. I
asked them then how about I use the spare capacity of
their ovens, I am from Khayelitsha and you can call it
community development. They said they would need
time to think about it and they would get back to me
because my approach took them off guard. I went back
to them again and I told them I am still looking for that
community development, I am from Khayelitsha, you
people are giants here and I am looking for an
opportunity to grow. I told them I am not coming to
them as a supplier, but a baby that needed to be
nurtured by them. They said since they can see that I
am persisting, they will give me what I want; let us give
it a try. That is where I got about R60 000 of profits
because I had no overhead, no rent and I had a shelf at
Spar and I was just baking from their facility. On the
other hand, I still had five bicycles and the people were
still selling for me so business was good. It was after a
year where I saw I had made enough profits for me to
branch out. I do not want this bread to be associated

with Spar or one day they replicate the same thing. I saw that it would get to a position or point where they could easily take over. Yes, they did not know the process because we did our premixes at home and by the time we went to Spar, we had everything ready. They knew the process, but did not know what goes into the bread. I started to get funding from companies, the media also helped to make people acknowledge us. The coverage from Forbes was a big one as I was listed as one of the 30 under 30 people to have come up with a great idea in Africa. Even SAB came to us and they gave us R70 000 and that brought our total of cash at hand to R130 000. That was sufficient to build our own express containerised bakery, which we know for a fact would be ours; it is an asset. I can say that one day if I decide to sell the business, I can count those assets unlike using Spar's facility where I would not be able to evaluate the share price. Thus far, we have our own express bakeries and supply seven Spar stores.

===*in terms of expanding, where do you see yourself going to*===

I am going back and forth. I was in Pretoria last week and the week before that I was in Durban; investments. There are a number of venture funding companies, which are interested in buying shares. I am still considering if we need to sell shares to grow the business or we continue and build it using grants, because that is possible as well. In Pretoria, Transnet and SAB are offering R400 000 to businesses and ideas that are unique and innovative. I am one of the finalists and once we get that we can scale up, capacitate the business, and have the capacity to supply more retail stores.

===*Lufefe you mentioned a number of times that you were turned down when you wanted funding and also the incident with Spar. Normally we have those negative people that do not see the idea materialising, how you navigated your way through this* ===

I will not lie I had a very supporting family and I do not know why, but it was such a blessing. By that time, I had graduated from the Raymond Ackerman Academy and they were expecting I would go and find a job. In as much as they did not pressure me, they saw the passion that I am not going anywhere. I think when they see that you are not testing waters they will see the passion. My mom was working as a domestic worker living in Barcelona squatter camps; at least she was working and getting something at the end of the month. I would come in as a child like any other child and say I need a plate of food. Sometimes my mother would go to the extremes of even borrowing money because she saw that my problem was getting enough ingredients. I needed ingredients every day and whatever I was getting was not enough. The demand was growing and I needed to scale up because I needed 1kg of baking flower at first and then I was sitting with

12.5kg. That was a bit of a hustle because sometimes I would need 5kg and sometimes 12.5kg. Every time my mother got paid and bought things, she would buy 12.5kg of brown flower for me. She was supportive; I do not know why hence I say it was really a blessing.

===*is there any person you could call your mentor when you look back at your journey*===

My community and the problems of my community mentored me. There was also a gentleman that inspired me by inviting me over when I was hustling. I would tell him that I am facing these challenges and I do not know what to do. He was running a successful business and he would ask me to meet him at Vida Café. I would make means to get to town by means of a train and arrive at Vida Café in Green Market Square, thinking that I will be sitting inside Vida Café. I would find him sitting on stones outside and he would be telling me the stories of hustling. I would go there thinking that he would give me at least R300 to help me out and he would be telling me stories. He was running a successful business and driving a good car; he would take me to the ATM, withdraw money and put it in his wallet. I could see the money; I could see the numbers on the screen too. He would look at me and say Lufefe I can see now you are doing good, the next meeting is on the second of next month. I would go back with no cash from him, I would have to take a train and sometimes negotiate with the train guards to let me in. I took that person as my mentor in as much as I was struggling at the time. I hated him a lot at the time and I did not understand that I could tell a person all my problems and yet they do not offer any assistance. Suddenly I thought this person is inspiring me that I needed to work hard to get those numbers, so yes he was in his own way my mentor.

===*you mentioned earlier on that you used to get up early at 03:00, how are your days like today*===

I wake up at 05:00 now and I have bakers baking through the night and during the day. So I wake up around 05:00 just to double check that everything is going well.

===*What advice would you share with upcoming entrepreneurs*===

Get out of your comfort zone, force your mind to think and when you force your mind to think, go to your community and look around. Annotate the problems of the community or the society. The problems of the community are business ideas and the solutions you will be coming up with will not only take care of the community, but also put bread on the table. As for my case I was trying to impact by going to the garden and help those old ladies, at the end of the day I got a business idea from that garden. They are now also my business partners, I am getting organic spinach from them for only R3 a bunch. You need to get out there and force your mind to think, be the change maker. Stop thinking about making money that is where you are not going to think.

===*what would you say is the most valuable lesson you have learnt on your journey*===

I have learnt to be humble and it is important to learn from others. It is important for entrepreneurs to network. I learnt to use what I have and not complain about the situation, find ways to overcome the problems and solutions will come abundantly to you. Off course, there are other lessons, but those are the key things I learnt.

------------------------------END------------------------

I remember reading about Lufefe and the "spinach bread" one evening from a friend's Facebook status. I love spinach, but I could not imagine what spinach bread would taste like. Anyway, I contacted Lufefe one morning and he was one of the most humble people I have ever come across. By then I had overcome the fear of contacting a stranger to request an interview, but the signs of anxiety were still there. Lufefe was able to do the interview within 5 days and I was totally chuffed about meeting him. On the day of the interview, I set out to his bakery so I could first have a taste of his products before meeting him and my imagination just ran wild. The muffins were delicious and before I could get to taste the bread, it was almost time for the interview. I got to his office about 5 minutes early and he was already outside on his way to meet me. The office was situated in a shared office space where a number of entrepreneurs new and old were sitting. This was something new to me at time and soon learnt that it was slowly becoming a trend in Cape Town. At the age of 23 Lufefe had already managed to draw quite a lot of media coverage and this had helped his business to grow also. I could not help but notice that the location of the business itself contributed to this, we have seen delis and bakeries come and go in some suburb areas. He mentions later that starting the business where he did, is what made him reach out to those areas that rejected him when his company was still nothing but an idea. Many people would rather start a business in a fancy suburb than in a township, here I pick up one of the valuable lessons from Lufefe. Essentially, the business was unique where it was started, a bakery is not unique, but his model was unique. It managed to draw attention and set the company in the right direction. From the word go Lufefe manages to catch my attention when he mentions the word unique and how the world would then follow people who come up with these unique ideas. I imagined how people might have doubted his idea in the beginning. Months after the interview I still managed to drive 80km to go and buy Lufefe's bread and muffins that alone indicates how unique what he has come with is, if it does not indicate how good the bread is.

At times when we evaluate our situations in life, we look for all the bad or negative things and mostly never doing nor learning anything from it. Lufefe became a vegetarian because he was getting paid with vegetables all the time, he accepted where he was at the time and did something about it. Another point is that in accepting the situation, we start to think clear and understand better that we need to start somewhere. This is shown by how Lufefe went to volunteer at a community garden and only received vegetables as some kind of compensation. Today we do not want to accept that to achieve great things we have to start little and at times start with nothing. If Lufefe was not so humble to start volunteering in that community garden, we would not know him for who is today. Then I again I like the simplicity and how passionate he is when he speaks about Popeye, the cartoon character. There is a saying that goes "in every man there's a child that wants to come and play, sometimes it's best to let him come out." This brought about the idea of promoting spinach like it has never has been before from spinach bread, smoothie and muffins. Even though Lufefe knew he had to start where he is, he knew the limitations as well in a sense that he could not bake the bread where he was staying. In understanding his limitations, he is able to approach his neighbour for help. I was also impressed by his thinking style, which for me goes back to looking at what one has and then working towards getting what you do not have. He managed to go online and learn about using every bit of information to get the desired outcome. Again in accepting where he is, Lufefe understands that he is David and the competition is Goliath that allows him to use a different strategy. This is shown again when he mentions he had to start with one product that was highly consumed so the business can have good cash flows I think in the whole interview Lufefe demonstrates a vast amount of courage, determination and discipline through many ways. One is where he continued to use the neighbour's bakery for 6months in the early hours and still have enough energy to go sell his bread to people.

After the interview, I had the opportunity to chat Lufefe for close to an hour about business and life in general, particularly the challenges thereof. Lufefe told me about his attempt to get into varsity and some of the local colleges and because his English marks were not good, he was rejected. He shared how he would go and beg to be accepted and this was ignored. Today he is invited to lecture MBA students on generating an original business idea. I found that I had a lot in common with him and he suggested that I watch the movie Catch Me If You Can starring Leonardo Dicaprio. Lufefe believes that there is nothing we cannot achieve if we truly set our minds to it.

CHAPTER 5

There Were Lessons

"Break away from the box confining you. Positive dreamers do not follow the status quo. They keep raising the standard of the bar higher and higher. Raise the bar."

— Israelmore Ayivor

My journey has been an interesting one from the start of writing this book to finally rounding up the last few pages. At the start, I was filled with excitement and thinking what could go wrong with writing a book as compared to starting a company. I was wrong and I am often wrong, a lot could go wrong. It has been months after resigning from fulltime employment and running around trying to find my feet. I have had to knock on doors of people of which some were celebrities and plead my case to get interviews. I have been reject over 11 times to get here, at one time I was rejected 5 minutes before a scheduled interview and when I felt like quitting, I was reminded of the first 4 interviews I had done.

When I set out on this journey, I wanted to prove that it is possible to break the barriers we have been subjected to and this proved to be true. Education is nothing but a tool to Think & Apply, which we have all been equipped with, not a tool for living from salary to salary. However, the way that education is imparted leaves many with some paralysis. I have heard many people, some very close to me claiming that they are frustrated at their current jobs and would leave if they could. I have also heard many people who complain that they hold a certain qualification and they cannot find work. Other people will put the blame on their upbringing and would blame it for their current circumstances. I have read about a number of people on websites and blogs looking for funding, some would start a business if only they just had enough cash or savings. We could blame these people or we could look for a solution. Society has embedded one thing on them, that is to walk life in a straight line, and that has worked for a few and has left a number of people in the cold. If these people do not meet the standards society expects them to, society will judge them. Education continues to tests people on what education thinks they should excel in, but not what they really excel in. I have met individuals who were very frustrated with their jobs and every time they thought of leaving, they would first compile a spreadsheet that made the power grid flicker, trying to work out their expenses. These people have been told to calculate and weigh the risk at all costs. A typical example is that of a man, I met a decade ago and all this time he kept on telling me how he would like to do mountain biking one day. I have fancied this myself from the time I started earning an income. Ten years later the man bought a mountain bike and this would see him live his dream of 40 years; the only problem is that during those 10 years he had undergone a knee operation. Ultimately, what this meant was that the man could never go cycling again. We have two roads to walk and they both have a destination. The one road is safe and you will end up pretty much where you started, but you skip a lot of check points in your life; you skip a lot of dreams. The other road is not safe and you end up with much more than you started with; you live your life to the fullest.

All these people have one or two things in common. (a) Fear and emotion controls them (b) they cannot tap into their creative part of the brain. It is evident in many ways that the interviewed people have broken this pattern and have regained their own way of thinking.

- Delane Zwane – had to choose between a secure job at Transnet and starting his own company.
- Igor Marinkovic – had to decide if he was going to listen to friends when they warned him about investing in the area he bought his first property
- Lynette Barnes– had to answer questions about her really leaving the old job.
- Wongama Baleni– made a decision to drop out of school to assist his mother and once again made a decision to leave his first job that paid well.

- Lufefe Nomjana– volunteered at a community garden at young age where most young people would not want to work.
- Langa Mbulawa – recalled how tough it was for him to leave his job, fear of the unknown.
- Reuben Riffel – made the choice between two jobs he was offered and could have walked away when the restaurant he was to work in was not complete.
- Sizwe Nzima – left the law class that he found to be boring and went on to follow his dream. Even when faced with accusations that he was selling people's medication, he found a way around it.

A farmer I once came across once shared the following and he called it the reason why most people will never realise their dreams: imagine that we were chickens in a chicken yard. The one end of the yard is covered with an electric fence and the hawks cannot get in. The problem is that there is less food and every chicken has to share in that safe environment. The other side of the yard there is a stockpile of corn and there is no electric fence, it is completely open. Which side would you choose, the safe end where you have to share, or the open end with plenty of food and just keep looking over your shoulder every now and then for the hawk.

We are all faced with this dilemma. I imagine the interview with Greg Heasley where he had to ask for money from his bother when things did not go so well. He found his feet after the incident and went back in search for greener pastures overseas once again. Now at that point in time, most people would be told they are insane if they go back there. On the day of writing this part, I was chatting with a colleague who was sharing with me war stories of people who have failed trying to search for independence. After each story I asked him, what happened to that person, and did they try something else again? The answer I got is that they gave up. A number of the interviewed people have failed at one point in their lives, but it is the bounce that matters.

Some of the interviewed people have been failed by the education system due to them not being able to show the required abilities. It is evident that they had more potential than required, but they were not tested where they showed strong skills. I have found that in order to be successful we have to search deep inside for our passion. I found also found that the skills or interest we have as kids play a crucial role in this.

Here are a number of key lessons learnt

1. **The Myths**
    -   You are now self-employed you do not have to wake up in the morning. As you can see with a number of the interviewed

people, they are up as early as 05:00 and some only go to bed at 02:00.

- If do not hold a qualification you cannot run a successful business. These interviews have shown that it is possible to do that, but you have to work harder.

- You have now made it you can stop working. A number of interviewed entrepreneurs have a net worth well over R1million and continue to work for a living.

2. Passion

- If you are to survive the journey, passion has to be the driving force, the fuel for the journey. I cannot recall how many days I have personally gone to bed depressed, but every days is a new day refuelled with passion. Find what you are truly passionate about and most of the time this is buried deep in our childhood days. We might not necessarily carry out the same skill we loved as kids, but we can adopt it to fit perfectly somewhere else.

3. The cloud of fear, doubt

- Fear and doubt are but a choice, they come naturally to one. Fear manifests itself where there is doubt. So when in doubt quickly find a way of dealing with it before it becomes fear. Lufefe Nomjana froze when he saw one of the big bakeries delivering bread, that was doubt, but he did not let it turn into fear.

4. **The decision to make**

- A number of the interviewed individuals had to make a serious decision at some point before they ventured into business. Some left their comfortable or promising jobs, others dropped out of school, a tough choice had to be made. The well-educated would advise that you save enough money before, that might work, but that does not guarantee anything. Make a choice that you will never have to look back on.

5. **Stand out**

- At some point, people will want to evaluate your sanity and that is fine. Bringing change is always questioned by people, it is that ability to remain there that makes them follow you.

6. **Direction**

- No one knows or shares your dreams or will even sympathise with you on your journey. Do not stress when the world does not seem keen to step out and help you. It is up to you to convince the world where you are heading.

7. **Personality**

   - Personality and attitude plays huge role. Finding something that fits your personality is key. You cannot be going out there with the intention to sell a product when you know that it does not match your style. For some it is easier to have a product that brings the customer to you.

8. **Attitude**

   - With all the interviewed entrepreneurs, their attitude is what led them to their success. The positive attitude in times of doubt, keeps them going and sometimes the decisions we make depend solely on the attitude.

9. **Discipline**

   - Without discipline, we are lost before we even start. Big companies operate on rules and some rules may not make sense, but they are built on discipline. Even the big retailers, they will open their doors at 08:00 regardless if there is a customer on the door or not. When things go sour, we continue doing what we were doing regardless and let discipline be our pivot.

10. **Skill and hard work**

   - At times, I juggle a number of things at once and will do the most I can, that could be seen as hard work. There are times when

I have to accept that a certain task needs skill more than hard work. This applies to employing people as well.

11. Patience

- Patience is one of the things practised and in some ways mentioned by many of the interviewed entrepreneurs. Things do not just kick off in the right direction once we open shop doors, they do so gradually. A lot could happen like losing partners, employees in the process.

12. Time-out

- More important than not, know when to take time out, when it is time to start something new. Some of the entrepreneurs started new ventures that did not work out so well and had to cut their losses. Some had to dissolve partnerships that did not work out well.

13. Though times

- Any business will experience tough times, some will sail through smoothly others will sink like the Titanic, while some may never start. Even big corporate companies experience tough times as Sizwe Nzima mentioned, in fact will have bigger problems.

14. Innovation

- A term that is loosely used by most people who are in business. We have a classic example of how Lufefe built something from nothing. Everything about his business he had to think hard and make means of building his dream. To be innovative requires a person to bring the child in themselves out. By child, I mean to do what no "normal" adult would do.

15. Ideas not a scarcity

- Simon Brown mentions this during the interview and if we can sit down and look around us, almost every problem that surrounds us is a business opportunity. The difference is that those who are willing to think are the ones that find them.

16. Find a Pivot

- Find something to be the pivot point that you can hold on to in stormy times. Wongama Baleni's family drove him more and that made him want to succeed. Delane Zwane was driven by the company name Delacom; it represented him and could not let it fail. When passion is not your pivot, find something else.

17. Problems are part of the mess

- Problems form part of the mess and there is not one problem that singles you out of the crowd. Simon mentions during the interview that there is no unique problem every problem you come up with, you are not the first person to come up with. Delane also mentions that if there is a problem there is a solution.

18. Intellectual Capital

- In as much as capital is required, the amount also largely depends on what ideas you come up with. If you are going to aim to build a spaceship, you might never get started. Force the mind to think of the smaller things.

19. David & Goliath Story

- At some point, we are going to have to face competition and knowing ourselves better will make us come out better. Simon Brown could have built his own website as he mentioned, but with JustOneLap he needed to have someone else build the website he wanted. Lufefe Nomjana approached the big retailer so he could bake from their premises. This allowed him to take advantage of his competitor's strong points.

20. Acceptance

- Important to accept when the course you have taken is not conducive to your course.

Only through accepting your current circumstances can you truly be aware of the weaknesses and strength. Only in acceptance are you able to think clearly without false thoughts clogging your mind. You become aware of the possibilities and as well as the limitations. Sizwe Nzima had to accept that he got bored in law. Most people want to start from the top and no one wants to start from the bottom. In this way even when his grandparents sent him to collect their medication, he did not refuse. Through accepting what he had to do, he found a business idea.

21. Solutions to problems

- There are unique businesses and there are original business ideas. Unique business ideas could be something like opening a filling station right in the middle of 200square km desert. Some of the businesses that came out of the interviews were unique and not original. An original business is coming up with something that has never been done been before. Nonetheless, some were solutions to existing problems. Lufefe wanted to change the way people lived in terms of health. Simon Brown believed that he needed to get JustOnelap to everyone out there and help people manage their money better.

22. Procrastination

- Procrastination is a storage facility for regrets, the more we procrastinate the more we fill up that facility. Holding on to the crystal ball waiting for a future that may never come when all that is crystal clear is in the review mirror.

PERSONAL REFLECTION

It would not be appropriate for me to end off the book without taking time to reflect on myself also, in what I have learnt. Firstly, it does not matter where one comes from and how little they have, it does not mean that determines where they are going. That is one of the things I try to apply daily dealings. I can be frustrated in the morning with things not going well, but how I choose to end my day is up to me. Secondly, I had to contact a number of people, some famous TV celebrities; these were people that have never heard of my company nor me at the very least. They were humble enough to allow me to their houses and offices; they did this with the hope of changing other people's lives out there. At times where I was rejected, I was always reminded of these individuals and that kept me going. One can only try to do something and when things do not work out, try again. Thirdly, it is evident in the interviews that we all know what we want to do with our lives from a very young age and we need an education system from home to school that allows us to grow that passion instead of killing it. I know there are number of people who are frustrated with their careers, lives and I say to you all, you are not alone, but you and only you can decide how you want to remember your life.